"Every day is a bonus!" —Jim McConkey

WHISTLER
AGAINST ALL ODDS

BY MICHEL BEAUDRY

MOUNTAIN SPORTS PRESS

BOULDER, COLORADO USA

Whistler: Against All Odds

Published by Mountain Sports Press

Distributed to the book trade by:
PUBLISHERS GROUP WEST

Copyright © 2002 Michel Beaudry

Bill Grout, *Editor-in-Chief*
Michelle Klammer Schrantz, *Art Director*
Alan Stark, *Associate Publisher*
Annie W. Krause, *Photo Editor*
Scott Kronberg, *Associate Art Director*
Chris Salt, *Production Manager*
Andy Hawk, *Sales Representative*
Megan Selkey, *Production Designer*

Whistler/Blackcomb®
is a registered trademark of Intrawest Corporation
at Whistler/Blackcomb.

All rights reserved.
No part of this book may be reproduced, stored in a retrieval
system, or transmitted, in any form or by any means, electronic,
photocopy, or otherwise, without the prior written permission
of the publisher, excepting brief quotations in connection with
reviews written specifically for inclusion in magazines,
newspapers, or online.

ISBN 0-9717748-2-X
Library of Congress Cataloging-in-Publiscation Data applied for.

Printed in Canada by Friesens Corporation

Prepress by Westphal West, Boulder, Colorado

Author's note: I make no claims to having written a
"comprehensive" history of Whistler. Rather, I've tried to
provide the reader with a multi-voiced mountain story in
which the whole, hopefully, is greater than the sum of
its parts. Enjoy.

A subsidiary of:

929 Pearl Street, Suite 200
Boulder, CO 80302
303-448-7617

To Gabriel and Suzanne,

for ensuring their four boys

had skis on their feet

from the moment they could walk.

CONTENTS

ACKNOWLEDGMENTS

Over the last 20 years I've been lucky enough to sell dozens of my Whistler stories to periodicals and newspapers around the world. Many of the themes developed in this book first saw the light of day in those articles. From *SKI* Magazine to *The New York Times*, from *Snowboard Life* to Canada's *Globe and Mail*, I've had the great good fortune of working with some of the most respected editors and wordsmiths in the business. To all the editors who've bullied, cajoled and encouraged me to write better, I'd like to say thanks. For when all is said and done, you're only as good as your team. ¶ I'd also like to thank my teammates on this project: Bill Grout, Michelle Schrantz, Chris Salt and Annie Krause at Mountain Sports Press. Without their help, this book would never have been published. ¶ In writing this kind of book, it becomes quickly apparent how much of a community project it is. And the Whistler community was incredibly supportive of my efforts. I'd like to thank Stuart Rempel and Kim Muller at Whistler/Blackcomb for their help and encouragement, Ed Pitoniak at Intrawest for his incisive critiques in the book's early stages and GLC manager Mike Varrin for just being there when I needed an ear to bend. I'd also like to thank Jinny Ladner, Paul Matthews and Drew Meredith for their help in understanding Whistler's critical transitions. ¶ One of Whistler's unsung heroes, Bob Barnett has been publishing a weekly newsmagazine, the *Whistler Pique*, for many years. Quiet and unassuming, Barnett has nonetheless provided a steady voice and a clear vision for the young community. Keep it up, Bob. ¶ Things can get pretty crazy writing a book. Whenever I needed to disappear into the backcountry for a few hours of sanity, I could always count on my good friend, Rob Boyd, to find time in his busy schedule for another B&B adventure. Most of all, I want to thank my spouse and partner, Wendy Ladner-Beaudry for putting up with me for over two decades. Her love has been the guiding light of my life. And to my daughters, Maya and Jenna, thanks for keeping me on my toes. ¶ Finally, the photographers whose work appear in this book are among the best in the world. They do incredible things with their cameras. I salute them all. This is their book too.

Published Sources

Books
Around the Sound — A History of Howe Sound-Whistler by Doreen Armitage
The Whistler Story by Anne McMahon
Vancouver/Garibaldi Olympic Bid Book for XII Winter Olympic Games
The Whistler Handbook by Bob Colebrook, Kevin Raffler and Jennifer Wilson
Whistler — History in the Making published by the *Whistler Pique*
The Whistler Outdoors Guide by Jack Christie
Sea to Ski Country by John Bartosik
Vancouver by Eric Nicol
Whistler: Changing Images by Brian Smith

Essays
"A History of the Development of Whistler Mountain Area" by Jinny Ladner

Author Michel Beaudry

AGAINST ALL ODDS

INTRODUCTION

WHISTLER

Everyone in the ski business in those days said it was impossible. Too big. Too stormy. Too isolated, they argued.

And it was a tough argument to counter. Lost in the Coast Mountains of British Columbia, perched on the very

edge of the Pacific Ocean—and with no services and no roads linking it to anywhere else—Whistler Mountain in

the early 1960s appeared far from ideal as a site for a future ski resort.

At least that's what the "experts" all thought. And according to the conventional wisdom of the time, they were right.

But Whistler's destiny has never been to conform to conventional wisdom.

For despite all its apparent drawbacks, Whistler had terrain. Lots of terrain. Big, juicy slopes that dropped nearly

a vertical mile to the valley floor. It also had a high-alpine zone more extensive than anywhere else on the continent. And hundreds of acres of old-growth forests just begging to be explored. And snow. So much snow. Deep and thick and consistent.

Up in the high country, winter lasted from October until June. On the glaciers draped around Whistler's peak, you could ski all year round, if that was your pleasure.

To Franz Wilhelmsen and his cohort of mountain enthusiasts, that was enough. Damn the naysayers, he said. They would go ahead and build a network of ski lifts on Whistler, regardless. The rest—roads and sewers and power stations and homes and lodges and restaurants—would sort themselves out with time. In a prophetic alpine twist on the *Field of Dreams* theme, Wilhelmsen and his team literally cut the resort out of the bush with the expectation that people—and money—would follow.

And it worked. Despite the experts' negative opinions. Despite the inclement weather. Despite, even, the vagaries of B.C.'s schizophrenic economy. Whistler kind of creaked along at first. No question. It even sputtered, backfired and almost died at one point. But it rallied. Went from backwater to world-class in two

decades. Grew on the shoulders of some of the greatest visionaries in the business—people like Al Raine and Nancy Greene, Hugh Smythe, Drew Meredith, Joe Houssian and Paul Matthews. And it thrived. Won prizes for design. Broke attendance records. Set new benchmarks for performance.

Today, Whistler is considered one of the premier mountain destinations in the world (only France's La Plagne sees more visitors in the winter). Featuring two mile-high mountains linked by a pedestrian-only village, Canada's great mountain experiment is the resort by which all others in North America are now judged. And it couldn't have happened without the participation of each and every individual profiled in this book.

For unlike so many of its U.S. counterparts—Vail or Squaw or Mammoth come to mind—the Whistler story is not about one man's vision brought to fruition. Rather, it is the story of the coming together of many visions. It's the tale of all the people who worked together tirelessly to develop a new mountain that would work both as a community and a resort. People who said "Why not?" instead of "Why?"

And that, in essence, is what this book celebrates. "No matter what anybody says now," says Hugh Smythe, pres-

Above: Big mountains. Deep snow. Long vertical. The view west from the summit of Whistler reveals a tantalizing skyline.
Opposite: Like lapiz stones on a necklace of jade, the region's lakes provide a fitting counterpoint to the local mountain scenery.

ident of the Resort Operations Group for Intrawest, Whistler/Blackcomb's parent company, "nobody really knew where the heck we were headed back then. We just had a bunch of strong-minded people committed to making this thing work. And somehow it did."

But the resort's business success is not all this book celebrates.

Call it blind luck, good fortune or a quirky combination of timing and location, but Whistler has also managed, over the years, to attract a group of talented and passionate residents whose competitive flair, high standards and easygoing style have added much to the local color. World-class athletes like Jim McConkey, Dave Murray and Stephanie Sloan set the tone in the early years; champions like Rob Boyd and Ross Rebagliati carried the Whistler torch in the '80s and '90s. Today it's the turn of kids who were conceived, born and grew up in the valley—like 2002 Europa Cup winner Britt Janyk or young halfpipe star Kai Petersen—to make their mark on the world stage.

But there are others too—lesser known but just as important—who have played huge roles over the years in bringing Whistler to life. From pioneer Myrtle Philip, whose 83 years bridged packhorse-travel to helicopters,

to Finnish logger Seppo Makkinen, who cut some of the most creative runs on the mountain; from artist and longtime Whistlerite Vincent Massey to pro patroller and community activist Cathy Jewett. They all had a hand in the formation of that elusive quality called "Whistler style."

For me as a writer, it is the dance of individual and environment that makes the story of a place so special. And to get a chance to develop the story of Whistler by telling the tales of its most colorful characters seems like a dream assignment to me. For in many ways, the Whistler story is one that I have witnessed—and lived— firsthand.

Like so many young skiers of my generation, I escaped to the mountains in the early '70s. In my case, it was almost literally an escape. As a scholarship athlete/student at Simon Fraser University in Vancouver, I had no intention of dropping out of school and moving to the mountains. Besides, I had no money for such frivolous things as skiing. My nose was pressed hard against the grindstone, and my sights were set firmly on "making my mark."

But all that changed during a fateful meeting with legendary big-mountain skier Jim McConkey. A friend of my father's, Jim was busy recruiting keen young

Opposite: **Joffrey Lake.**
Below: **A gateway to some of the most spectacular alpine terrain in North America, Whistler Village also boasts a surprisingly urban lifestyle.**

skiers for his burgeoning ski school at Whistler. Out of the blue he asked me if I wanted a job. I didn't even think about the answer. I just nodded. Twenty-four hours later I had quit school, quit the swim team, moved out of my Vancouver apartment and was riding Whistler's Big Red chair with my first class. I didn't miss a day of skiing from that point on until the lifts finally shut down on May 24 of that year.

It was a life-changing moment. Not even out of my teens yet, I experienced something of an epiphany during that first winter at Whistler. In short, it soon became all too evident to me that I would never be able to integrate into the nine-to-five routine of mainstream society. And I also realized I really didn't want to, anyway. I wanted adventure in my life. I wanted challenges. And I certainly didn't want security. Fortunately for me, I was surrounded by dozens of talented, well-adjusted kids—and adults—who thought exactly the same as I did. We skied, we explored, we played—and we dreamed up new and exotic ways of "making a living."

Admittedly, I could have never dreamed up the scenario of my future career as a globe-trotting writer (and who would want to anyway?). But it works. And it works, I believe, because I stayed true to the passions that I discovered in myself during that first season at Whistler. I have never led a nine-to-five existence. And I've survived more than my fair share of adventures and challenges. I have an interesting job, a growing family and I still get more ski days at Whistler than I deserve. So far so good, as they say.

Did my first youthful winter on the slopes of Whistler, in some way, set me on my writer's path? I'm not sure, but I know it didn't hurt. As a source of inspiration, Whistler's bigger-than-life environment has always been there for me. I wouldn't be the same person I am now if I hadn't accepted Jim McConkey's job offer on that cold and snowy January day in 1974.

So this book, in many ways, is a labor of love—a tribute to this place called Whistler and to the people who proudly call themselves Whistlerites. Over the last few months, I've had the great good fortune to sit down with dozens of friends and acquaintances and reminisce about the past. We talked about the early years, when there were only a few lifts on this huge mountain and powder snow could be found on just about any day of the winter. We talked of our sense of somehow being blessed for having experienced those days—and being forever changed by those experiences. We talked about the '80s and the coming of Blackcomb and the crazy politics surrounding the building of the new village. And, of course, we all had opinions about the economic recession that hit just as Blackcomb opened its doors and the near collapse of the whole enterprise in 1981. We talked about the real-estate madness that consumed the valley and Whistler's gradual ascension to king-of-the-hill status in North America. Of its growing reputation overseas. Of its youthful workforce from Australia and England and Japan.

But most of all we talked about people. The people who had touched us. Inspired us. Pushed us to do the right thing. We marveled, in fact, at the number of early Whistlerites who subsequently made an impact on the global ski and snowboard business. The movers and shakers, the innovators, the risk-takers. We also talked about those who had left us too soon—Dave Murray and Trevor Petersen and Lumpy Leidel and Brett Carlson, to name but a few.

We laughed and cried. Sighed, wiped a tear or two away and laughed some more.

In its nearly 40 years of existence, Whistler has somehow always managed to beat the odds. Still imposingly big and unmanageably stormy, still too isolated and too hard to reach for some people, Whistler will remain an enigma for those who love well-heeled, sunny ski hills that aren't too intimidating. But for people who love their mountains in XL size (with all the weather and variable conditions that entails), Whistler will always reign supreme.

And for that, I'm truly grateful.

Michel Beaudry

Summer 2002

Opposite: **The author at work. When the storm breaks and the upper mountain opens, Whistler/Blackcomb becomes a powder playground.**

CHAPTER 1
MYRTLE PHILIP

Everyone loved Myrtle. In the fast-growing '70s and '80s, she was a touchstone to the past. A bit of living history

for our young Whistler community. But she was more than that, too. For in a place where most people's roots

had barely settled into the rough mountain soil, Myrtle Philip was confirmation that you could make it here if

you really wanted to. And that you could do it with style.

After all, hadn't Myrtle drawn tourists up here decades before roads and electricity arrived? Hadn't she lived

here since 1914 and never regretted a moment of it? Couldn't she fish and hunt and hike as well as any man?

And couldn't she manage a remote lakeside lodge and cook for 30 guests on a wood stove at a moment's notice?

Above: **Garibaldi Lake. The sublime pleasures of a Whistler summer are as much appreciated today as they were a century ago.**
Opposite: **Canoeing on Alta Lake in the 1920s. People came for the fishing. But they stayed because of Alex and Myrtle Philips' hospitality.**

"God's greatest cook," they called her.

Strong and funny and graceful and wise, Myrtle had the natural country charm of a born storyteller—and the pioneering history to back up her words. More than anything, though, she had a deep and abiding love for her mountain home. You could see it in her eyes. You could feel it in her smile. There was nowhere else she'd rather be than right here. Whistler, as she'd known it for over half a century, was where she belonged.

And in that way she wasn't all that different from the ski bums, eccentrics and alpine dreamers who had been trickling into the valley. "It's been a lot of fun to see this place take off," she'd often say. "These young folk today have a love for life that I really admire."

Already in her mid 70s when the first ski lifts were erected on the slopes across from her place on Alta Lake, Myrtle Philip spent the final 20 years of her life surrounded by the maelstrom of a fast-developing ski resort. Yet through it all, she remained unflappable. It never seemed to bother her. She was never bitter or negative or sour about the "coming of progress."

And she never made excuses about her own lack of "vision." "People keep asking me why we didn't look into this downhill skiing thing so we could attract more visi-tors in the winter," she would say. "But we always thought that the equipment was so expensive that no one would want to do it. To see it all so changed now is like a dream."

Watching her at civic gatherings over the years—being fussed over by mayors and prime ministers, ski stars and administrators—I often tried to imagine what she was really thinking behind her placid public mask. Was she really happy about the valley's transformation from quiet backwater to busy mountain resort? Or did she pine for the good old days when the local home-steaders climbed "Whistle" Mountain to pick berries on its south-facing slopes?

She never said. By the time she passed away in 1986—at the age of 95—Myrtle Philip had become a Whistler legend. The local elementary school was named in her honor. And the site where Myrtle and her husband, Alex, had built their lakeside lodge was turned into a municipal park. The woman who had first set eyes on this place walking alongside a packhorse—and had survived long enough to soar over it in a helicopter—had left an indelible mark on the valley she so dearly loved. And that's the way it should be, says Whistler patroller Cathy Jewett. "She was an inspiration to me,

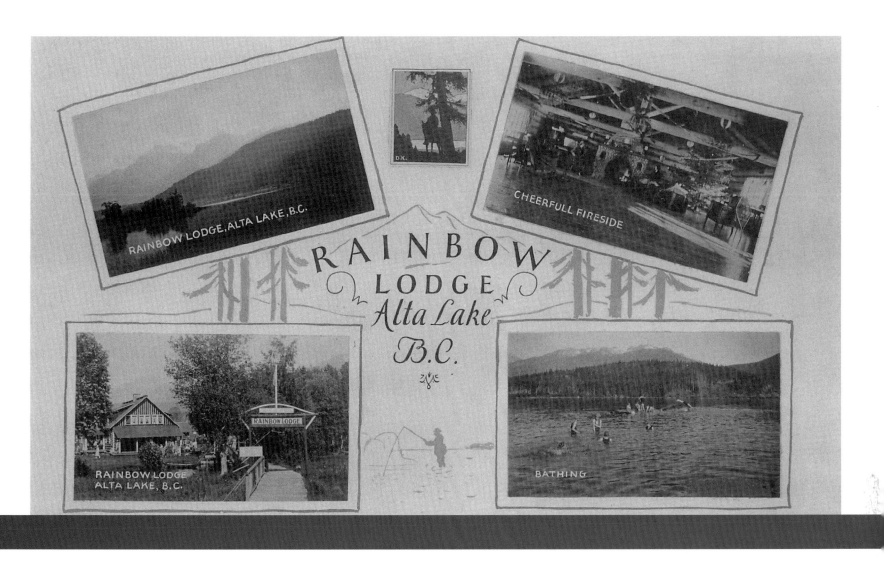

for sure. She had chutzpah, you know? She was the kind of woman I've always admired."

It took a long time for the first European to reach the northwest coast of North America. It wasn't until the dying years of the 18th century, in fact, that the coastline was even surveyed. And then, in quick order, this rich land was plundered. Spurred on by an Asian obsession with sea-otter pelts, British, Spanish and Russian fleets ravaged the coast with barbaric abandon and managed to nearly eradicate the thick-furred sea mammals in just a few decades.

As for penetrating into the rugged and inhospitable-looking land, it took 50 more years—and the lure of gold—before white men ventured into the Interior in any numbers. And it was a painful and difficult process at best.

"It was the most arduous trip [of my life]," wrote naval lieutenant Richard Mayne of his 1860 journey in search of a new route from the Coast to the gold fields of the Interior. One of the first Europeans in history to travel up Cheakamus Canyon and through Whistler Valley, Mayne recorded his thoughts on his surveying trip in his daily journal. Later published as *Four Years in British Columbia and Vancouver Island*, it reveals in detail just how brutal the adventure was. The party was assailed by swarms of blood-thirsty mosquitoes every day of the trip.

Beaten down by feet-sucking swamps and clothes-tearing devil's club. Stymied at every turn by thick bush and impassable mountain creeks. On good days, the expedition barely covered one kilometer an hour.

Unbeknownst to Mayne, the native people had been trekking over the high passes of the Coast Range for thousands of years. Linking up animal trails at first, they had devised elaborate—and ingenious—ways of getting through this difficult country in order to hunt, fish and exchange trade goods with neighbors.

Midway through their trip, Mayne's party was fortunate enough to stumble onto one of the natives' major mountain byways. This one connected the coastal Squamish tribe to their Lillooet counterparts on the other side of the range. At this point, things seemed to have improved greatly for the young adventurer. He describes stopping for breakfast and relaxing in the grass by the side of a lake at the north end of a high mountain pass. "Finding that the Indians knew no name for it," he wrote in his journal, "I called it Green Lake, from the remarkably green color of the water."

The Pemberton Trail, as it would eventually become known to white settlers, had been used for trade by both native groups since the beginning of time. The network

Opposite: **The snow was deep. And the route was very steep. But in 1914, the PGE still managed to push a rail line through the Coast Mountains to Alta Lake and the Interior of B.C.** Above: **Before World War II, Alta Lake was considered the biggest Canadian tourist destination west of Banff.**

LOGGING AT WHISTLER

From the late 1920s to the 1960s, logging was the lifeblood of Alta Lake. And much of its economic success was due to the terrain-defying railway line that the PGE had built from the mountains to tidewater in Squamish back in 1914. "The line was a marvel of surveying and construction," writes historian Doreen Armitage in her book *Around the Sound*. "[It was] accomplished by men without modern equipment or aerial survey methods, through terrain that had always been considered too mountainous to maintain the low grades required by a railway."

First conceived as a rail link to the Interior of B.C. and the lucrative gold fields that were being exploited there in the late 19th century, the PGE quickly turned its sights to the more accessible "green gold" that grew, seemingly without limit, on either side of its rail line.

The earliest loggers to establish themselves between Alta Lake and Green Lake were small one- and two-man pole-cutting teams (often called gypo outfits) who would fell, trim and skid their logs to special rail sidings with the help of teams of horses. There, their long, straight logs (destined for work mostly as telephone poles) would be picked up by the train on its southern journey back to Squamish. The work was brutally hard and the small teams would come and go from season to season. Individuals could sustain themselves on this kind of work for a while, but most were beaten down by the demanding conditions and limited return on their efforts.

The first real commercial operation in the area started in 1926, when the Barr brothers built the valley's first sawmill on a point of land in Green Lake called Parkhurst. At its peak in the late 1920s, the mill employed up to 60 men and produced 35,000 board feet of lumber per day. For years, Parkhurst was the PGE's biggest client, transporting a carload of timber a day. When the mill burned down in 1937, the operation was forced to shut down and all work stopped. It wasn't until after World War II, in 1945, that new Parkhurst owners, Byron Smith and his son Jerry, decided to rebuild a smaller mill and resume operations. It continued to be profitable until 1956, when it was finally dismantled for good.

By this time, other operations had moved into the Whistler Valley. Reflecting the ideology of their era, these operators viewed the vast stands of first-growth timber that crept up the mountains' flanks solely as a resource to be exploited— not necessarily one to be admired. "So they cut the trees and sold them without

regard to their visual desecration of the slopes," writes Ann McMahon in *The Whistler Story*. "Debris was dumped into the lakes without a thought for the fish. And forestry regulations required the [logging] slashes to be burnt." Ugly logging scars began to mar the valley's alpine scenery. Out-of-control slash fires often threatened the lives of hiking tourists. But the logging companies were bringing much-needed cash to an economically strapped region, and the dwindling summer tourism trade just didn't have the clout to control them.

With the coming of skiing to Whistler in 1966, that approach could no longer be sustained. And the ensuing clash between the logging and mountain-tourism factions soon came to a head. A bridge used by L&K Logging to access the lower slopes of Blackcomb Mountain (for which the company had a legal permit) was burned down by arsonists in 1974. Although no one was ever convicted of the crime, it served to drive an even bigger wedge between loggers and recreationalists in the valley. Pioneers like Laurence Valleau (of Valleau Logging), who had given so much of himself to the young community, felt totally betrayed and soon moved away.

The last nail in the Whistler loggers' coffin, however, came in the form of a letter that the B.C. deputy minister of forests sent on August 21, 1975, to L&K Logging. It mandated "no further commercial logging [to be allowed] in the Whistler-Blackcomb area." In effect, the ban applied to any cut block that was visible from either mountain, thereby eliminating pretty much any form of logging in the valley.

Left and above: **The trees were big and the forests were vast. Logging was a real adventure in the old days.**

Though the winter months saw few
tourists, the locals were not afraid
to try their hand at new sports.

of lakes at the top of the pass—Alpha, Nita, Alta and the aforementioned Green Lake—was considered the boundary lands between the two nations. To the south, the Squamish ruled. To the north was Lillooet land.

The young explorer was smitten by his surroundings. But although it was more beautiful than anything he'd seen yet in his travels, Mayne was also smart enough to realize that building a road to the interior here would be prohibitively expensive. He reported his findings back to his superiors in Victoria, and the region lapsed back into obscurity.

It was into this still-wild region that Myrtle Philip and her husband, Alex, first ventured on horseback in 1911. The Philips were originally from the coast of Maine. A jovial, easygoing man, Alex had opened a restaurant in Vancouver in 1905, and when things started looking good four years later, he had sent for his young fiancée, Myrtle Tapley. They married in 1910.

The Philips' Horseshoe Grill catered mostly to loggers—both local and transient—and was a popular place with hardworking single men. But even in the Horseshoe Grill, the squashed-nose bantam rooster who showed up one night for dinner dressed in fringed buckskins and wide-brimmed hat was something of a standout. Lonely for company, and slightly addled with booze, Mahogany John Millar was soon entertaining Alex with stories about a magical spot up in the mountains where he'd built himself a cabin. The fish were so abundant in the high lakes around his homestead, he said, that you almost had to beat them off with a stick!

It turned out that Millar had preempted some waterfront land just off the Pemberton Trail, on what was then called Summit Lake. ("There was another Summit Lake in B.C. already," Myrtle liked to explain, "so they changed the name to Alta Lake.") It was the most beautiful property in the world, Millar said. An ideal place for a fishing lodge. Only he wasn't much interested in that. He was much more into trapping and mineral exploration.

Millar was definitely a character. Cook, cattle-wrangler, trapper and jack-of-all-trades, the rough-hewn frontiersman was also a storyteller of some repute. He loved to tell the tale, for example, of the time when he caught a wolverine in one of his traps, "killed" it with his axe and then stuffed it in his bag—only to have it recover from the blow, eat through the pack and clamp its jaws securely on the seat of Millar's pants.

Alex was entranced by the old guy's stories. Before he knew it, he'd invited Mahogany John home to meet Myrtle. Either Millar was a great salesman, or Alex and Myrtle were both keen for a major life change. For the very next day they set off with him on a two-week fishing expedition to Summit Lake.

At that time, there was no road or railway to the north of Vancouver. To reach the foot of the Pemberton Trail, the Philips had first to board a ferry—the Bowena—for the one-day sail up Howe Sound to Squamish (then just a tiny village called Newport). From there, it was another two days on horseback before they'd even get the chance to see the lake.

"The trail was just a track, barely two feet wide," Myrtle would often recount to the local kids. "It ran roughly where the road is today, but it was covered with boulders and we had to pick our way over fallen logs and deep gullies. It was a very difficult ride."

But the destination was well worth the effort. "Remember—there'd been no logging yet in this area," she'd explain. "The mountains above Alta Lake were still all covered in old-growth forests. Huge cedars and giant firs. Snow still lay on the upper slopes. It was utterly beautiful."

And the fishing wasn't bad either. A neophyte before the Summit Lake trip, Myrtle was encouraged by her husband—already an accomplished angler—to try her hand at it almost immediately upon her arrival. She was skeptical at first. "I wasn't sure I was even going to like it." But Millar's fishermen tales had not been exaggerated. On her first cast, she caught a big, fat rainbow trout. "I never had so much fun," she'd say. "The water was so clear in those days you could see the fish coming for your bait."

Alex and Myrtle were hooked. They returned to Vancouver and the Horseshoe Grill and set about saving every penny they could. It took until 1913 for the young couple to raise the money they needed—$700—to buy 10 acres of waterfront land on Alta Lake. But they finally managed it. "It was a beautiful piece of property," she'd explain. "I knew it was worth every penny we invested in it." The prospector from whom they bought the place, a fellow named Charlie Chandler, had never seen so much money before in his life. "So he went right to town for a splurge. It must have been quite a splurge, because he came back dead broke."

So Chandler approached Alex once again and offered to sell him his remaining land—over 100 acres—at a much more reasonable price. "He took the money and disappeared into the bush again," Myrtle would tell her listeners. "I guess his last splurge was enough."

Even as a young bride, Myrtle had an air of quiet confidence about her that no amount of Victorian lace could camouflage.

On May 9, 1914, Alex, Myrtle, and her father and two brothers began construction on what would eventually become the most popular summer destination west of the Rocky Mountains: Alta Lake's Rainbow Lodge. "It was an enormous amount of work at first," she'd say. "No one today could even imagine how hard it really was."

But they kept at it. For their dream was fast becoming a reality. First they cleared the land. Then they built a little sleeping cabin on the slope above the main site. Finally they were ready to start building the lodge.

And it was a daunting task—even for Myrtle's father, an accomplished carpenter. Every log had to be hand cut with axe and saw, and then each had to be peeled individually. Every plank they used had to be cut—and planed—by hand. As for getting supplies, it was backbreaking work. Every nail, every bolt, every pane of glass had to be carefully transported over the Pemberton Trail on horseback. But somehow they managed. The roof was completed only days before the snow started to fly. For now, the interior could wait. At least they were sheltered from the elements.

The original Rainbow Lodge featured a big, airy dining room with a large kitchen in the corner. On either side of the main floor were bedrooms. Two more bedrooms and a dormitory were added on the second floor. Why the name Rainbow Lodge? "It was a dream we'd been chasing: It was our pot of gold," Myrtle liked to explain. "But it was the rainbow trout that brought us here."

Meanwhile, progress was slowly working its way up the valley. And once again, it was strictly due to the province's bountiful natural wealth. Up until the early 1900s, logging had remained pretty much a tidewater activity in British Columbia. After all, the pickings were so easy along the coast that no one felt any need to push farther inland. But soon the great belt of old-growth coastal forests that had greeted European travelers little more than a hundred years before had all but been depleted of commercial lumber. It was time to move.

Spurred on by the potential riches of the vast stands of timber found in the interior of the province, a group of investors had begun working on a scheme to push a railroad up the Pemberton Trail. Their goal was to build a line linking Squamish (and tidewater) to Prince George, in the far northeast of B.C. Preposterous, the experts said. The terrain was just too rough to make it a going concern. The plan was indeed an ambitious one. But the group appeared to have sufficient funds—and the vision—to pull it off.

Less than a year after the completion of Rainbow Lodge, the Pacific Great Eastern Railway line finally crested the pass at Alta Lake. In one summer, everything changed. What had hitherto been an isolated, hard-to-get-to mountain gem suddenly became far more accessible to Vancouver's burgeoning tourist trade. Now, an angler and his family could conceivably board the Union Steamship ferry in downtown Vancouver in the morning, transfer aboard the PGE train in Squamish in the afternoon and be having dinner at the Philips' lodge later that evening.

It was the PGE, in fact, that really put Rainbow Lodge on the map. For in the spring of 1915, the Philips were contacted by representatives of the railway company. "They wondered if we might entertain the idea of hosting a fishermen's excursion train planned for later that summer," Myrtle would say.

"Well, I never catered to anybody before, but I could cook, so we agreed to try it. I got busy planning menus, because all our supplies had to come in by packhorse or freight wagons."

When the day finally came, 25 fishermen got off that

Whether they were hosting 10 guests or 30 at Rainbow lodge, Alex and Myrtle always made sure everyone got his or their fair share of fish.

special train. Myrtle didn't have a clue what to do with them all. "We only had one boat and two rafts," she'd say. "But every one of those fishermen got a fish. And they went back home and told all their friends about Alta Lake." It was exactly what the owners of Rainbow Lodge needed. From that moment on, the Philips had all the business they could handle.

"We charged 40 cents per night in the early years," remembered Myrtle. "People thought that was a fair price for what we offered."

For the next 25 years, the Philips prospered. And people came from all over the world to sample their backcountry brand of hospitality. Together with their guests, they hiked and fished in the summer and cross-country skied and skated in the winter. For a few years, they even tried their hand at iceboating. "When I got the hang of it," Myrtle would recount, "I had a great time. It skimmed along at such speed."

The Philips owned saddle horses, too, and trail riding became a popular activity with the younger set. Alex—always a romantic—would take young couples on moonlit canoe rides down his "river of golden dreams" in order to prod Cupid a little. Myrtle even became something of a celebrity with Vancouver out-door writers. "Myrtle Philip is the best fisherman in the whole district," gushed one prominent scribe in a local fishing column. "She ties her own flies, and she can put a fly on a downstream wind like most people just dream about..."

Myrtle had dozens of stories from those years. And it didn't take much prompting to get her going. She loved to tell the one about the gentleman staying at the lodge who decided one day to wash his Sunday suit. Short of laundry soap, he decided, instead, to use gasoline. His suit now clean and spotless, the gentleman threw the used gasoline down the outhouse hole.

"Now, it was one of the old gent's habits to smoke cigars in the outhouse," she would recount, "so the next day—when he'd completed his business—he casually pitched his still-lit cigar down the outhouse hole." The explosion blew him right through the outhouse door, said Myrtle. "When people came out to see what had happened, he turned to them and exclaimed: 'It must have been something I ate.'" I can still hear her laughing happily at her own story.

Although she and Alex never had children—"I'm not sure I could have handled being a mother and taking care of the lodge," she once admitted—she did more

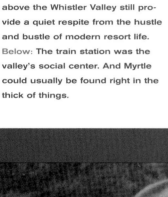

Opposite: The high-mountain lakes above the Whistler Valley still provide a quiet respite from the hustle and bustle of modern resort life. Below: The train station was the valley's social center. And Myrtle could usually be found right in the thick of things.

Given the growing reputation of Rainbow Lodge as a summer destination in the '20s and '30s, it should come as no great surprise that other guesthouses and lodges soon began to spring up on the shores of Alta Lake. These were mostly summer-only accommodations and built in the rough-hewn style of the B.C. backcountry. But what they lacked in modern amenities, they made up for in local charm.

Burt and Agnes Harrop were first introduced to the region as guests of the Philips. Overwhelmed by the beauty of the place, they bought their own "piece of heaven" in 1920 on a spectacular point of land just to the south of Rainbow Lodge. There, they built Harrop's Tearoom, a building with a large veranda overlooking the lake where Agnes would serve afternoon tea to her guests and then read their fortunes in the leaves left at the bottom of their cups.

Dick Fairhurst, a local logger and trapper, was really taken with the Harrop's location and bought the Tearoom and the surrounding land for $1,000 in 1945. His plan was to tear down the old Harrop buildings and replace them with a number of cottages on the point and rent them out to summer visitors. A year later, a new main building, Cypress Lodge, was completed, and he and his wife, Eunice, ran their operation successfully until 1972, when they sold their property to the Canadian Youth Hostel Association for $150,000.

Hillcrest Lodge was built by Jack Mansell in 1947 on the southeast side of Alta Lake. The post-war tourism business was booming during those years, and even though Hillcrest was much farther away from the rail line than Cypress or Rainbow, Mansell had little trouble filling his lodge during the summer months. In the early 1960s, when Franz Wilhelmsen began poking around in search of a new ski area location, he often stayed with the Mansells at Hillcrest Lodge, from which he and his climbing buddy Stefan Ples would mount their expeditions up the mountain.

The Mansells eventually sold Hillcrest to a group of Vancouver businessmen in 1965 who quickly renamed it the Mount Whistler Lodge. In the late '60s and '70s, it became one of the few social centers available to the new winter residents looking for a little camaraderie and spirits. Whether it was après-ski on Saturdays for the Vancouver crowd, or Wednesday night movies for the locals, Mount Whistler Lodge served an important function for the burgeoning community until the development of Whistler Village in 1980.

Russ Jordan was one of Alta Lake's true old-timers. Jordan, who first traveled through the region at the turn of the century on his way to the Cariboo gold fields, ran a coffee shop for years in a dilapidated roadhouse that he'd dragged up to Alta Lake from the PGE's abandoned Cheakamus camp farther south. When the old building finally burned down in 1930, Jordan decided to see the world and signed on with Canadian Pacific's Empress of Japan ocean liner as a barber. But Alta Lake's magic wouldn't let him go for long. He returned five years later and settled on a quarter section of land at the south end of Nita Lake (which, interestingly enough, encompassed much of what is now referred to as the Creekside area—on both sides of the highway). He built a main guesthouse and a bunch of smaller cabins around the lake and opened for business as Jordan's Lodge.

One last point of interest: In the early 1960s, Garibaldi Lifts negotiated with Jordan to buy his property. His quarter section of land was the ideal size for a base village, it had direct access to the rail line and to the highway, and it boasted a significant waterfront section as well. An agreement was reached, and the company quickly set about drawing up the necessary documents for the final sale. Unfortunately, Jordan died before the completion of the transaction and the property was eventually sold by his estate to another bidder. Who knows what Whistler would look like today had Russ Jordan managed to stay alive long enough for the sale to go through?

Left and above: **Rustic but friendly.**
Whistler lakefront in the 1930s.

Though lifts wouldn't grace Whistler Mountain for another half-century, Myrtle and her friends clearly enjoyed their skiing parties."

for the small mountain community than just about any-body else in the 60-year history of Alta Lake. She acted as midwife to countless pregnant mothers, and nursed and set the broken bones of any injured loggers or rail-way workers who staggered into the lodge. She also took care of much of the local business. She ran the post office for nearly 40 years (at the same annual salary of $600), lobbied the provincial government successfully to build a school in the valley in the early 1930s—and then served on the local school board with nary a missed meeting until she retired in 1970.

Myrtle and Alex sold Rainbow Lodge to Alex Greenwood in 1948 for $100,000. The Philips were get-ting older, and they weren't sure they had the energy to keep the old place going in the style they'd been accus-tomed to. Besides, things had changed in the interven-ing years. A number of other lodges had sprung up around the lake. And logging was a much bigger player

now. Rainbow just didn't have the draw it once had. Still, Myrtle was heartbroken when she finally had to move. "I never wanted to sell," she admitted. "And for a long time I was like a fish out of water, without a place to swim. But I eventually got over it."

The two moved to a little cabin on the west side of Alta Lake and continued to take advantage of their mountain surroundings until they were both well into their twilight years. They chopped their own wood, grew their own vegetables— and even ventured out onto the lake from time to time to see if they could tempt yet another monster rainbow onto their hooks. When Alex died in 1968 at the age of 86, people tried to encourage Myrtle to move into more modern accommodations. But she refused. "Why would I want to change the way I live now? I've lived a great life here in Alta Lake. And I'll continue to live it the way I want till the day I die."

And she did.

Below: **You could see it in her smile. Whether at 30 or 90, Myrtle Philip exuded a love of life that was as infectious as it was inspiring.** Opposite: **"Why would I want to change my life now?" Once she found her home, Myrtle never left.**

CHAPTER 2
FRANZ WILHELMSEN

There are few places in the world where mountains and ocean blend more seamlessly than the west coast of

British Columbia. And there are few places in the world as rugged. From Vancouver in the south to Prince Rupert

in the north stretches a thousand-mile coastline of brutal beauty. Pacific-driven storms strike with all-too-fre-

quent regularity here. Mist and fog play hide-and-seek in moss-covered trees; seagulls soar off thousand-foot

cliffs. It is not a particularly friendly place to humans—at least not at first glance.

This is a land of extremes, no doubt about it. But it's in those extremes that dwell the special charm of the

Coast Mountains. Narrow, glacier-cut fjords thrust deep into the hinterlands, flanked by 8,000-foot peaks

42

crowned with year-round snow. Forests of cedar and hemlock and fir push fingers of green high up the mountains' flanks. It's a land of granite and conifers, steep angles and deep waters. A place where the geography imposes its own conditions. Where salmon and orca and eagle and raven still rule.

It's a land that commands respect. Boater, skier or rock climber; paddler, hiker or mountaineer—it doesn't matter. You make a mistake here and the consequences are severe.

It's also as far west as you can go on this continent. And it tends to attract a hardy type of entrepreneur: adventurers, risk-takers and dreamers, more than businessmen. The kind with a lot of energy to burn and a lot of drive to expend.

Like Franz Wilhelmsen. "Everyone just laughed when we proposed our idea to them," he was fond of recounting in his Nordic-tinted English. "'Hah!' they said. The government, B.C. Hydro, the investment community, even the people of Vancouver. Build a ski area at Whistler? It would never work. We were all crazy for even thinking about it."

His story is what Hollywood films are made of. A member of the Royal Norwegian Air Force during World War II—and an outgoing, handsome officer at that—Franz met a vivacious young Canadian debutante while stationed in Toronto. The two immediately fell in love and got married. Turns out his new bride, Annette Seagram, was from one of the most prominent families in the country.

"That's one of the keys to this story," says a longtime acquaintance. "Franz was a guy with a lot of energy. And he was a bull for hard work. But he was also a very proud man. You always got the sense that he was trying to prove himself to the rest of the world. Trying to show that he was, indeed, a self-made man...You have to understand what it was like back then. Here was this young Norwegian émigré and a stranger to the Canadian establishment. He just wanted to show that he belonged."

The other key to the story is Annette herself. "She was my dad's biggest supporter," says their son, Phillip Wilhelmsen. "And his greatest ally. Her encouragement over the years carried him through many a rough spot. They were quite a team, in fact."

Franz and his bride soon were drawn to Canada's West Coast. It's not surprising. A land brimming with opportunities, coastal B.C. was much like the home the young man had left behind in Norway. Only bigger. Much bigger. And wilder, too. And with all sorts of possibilities. For someone with a little imagination—and a lot of energy—it was a match made in heaven.

Above: Black Tusk at sunset. It was scenery like this that convinced Wilhelmsen and his colleagues that Whistler Mountain had what it took to become a successful ski resort.
Opposite: Franz and Princess Marta, 1942. Never one to hesitate to take matters into his own hands, a young Franz darns socks in the company of Norwegian royalty.

Besides, leaving Toronto would allow the young entrepreneur to set his own agenda for the future. And for the proud Norwegian, that was probably just as important a consideration.

The Wilhelmsens set up house in Vancouver. Still very much a provincial backwater (in the eyes of genteel Toronto society), Vancouver in the mid 1940s was the booming gateway to B.C.'s northwest coast. And Franz jumped into the West Coast business world with both feet.

He first tried his hand at the shipping trade. "He ran a passenger/freight business," says another friend. "He bought a couple of b-class motor launches from the Canadian navy and set himself up to service the little sea-front communities strung along the coast of B.C. That's when he first got to really know his new home."

And he was smitten. But who wouldn't be by this magical seascape? Salmon on every cast. Oysters and crabs and prawns at arm's reach. And miles and miles of empty coastline. It was a land blessed by the gods. Stormy for sure. And rainy far too often. But then, how would those magnificent coastal forests thrive otherwise?

For a while, the business prospered. But the Union Steamship Company—which had interrupted its operation soon after the start of World War II—had no intention of letting this upstart take over the company's lucrative coastal trade. A few years after the termination of hostilities, they resumed their business. With deeper pockets and a bigger fleet, they just marched right in and took over where they'd left off. And just like that, it was over. Franz's coastal freight business was finished.

But Franz was not deterred. Over the next few years he would launch a number of risky new ventures—he developed a marina on Vancouver's North Shore, for instance, and built the first high-rise apartment in West Vancouver. But nothing really excited his passions. Nothing seemed to fit his talents. Still, he never stopped looking. Searching out new opportunities. Checking out new leads.

Then came the 1960 Olympics and Squaw Valley's coming-out ceremony. This is how Franz Wilhelmsen remembered it: "After the 1960 Games, a group from the Canadian Olympic Association (COA) traveled out to the West Coast to have a look around. They'd been very impressed by the way Alex Cushing and Squaw Valley had put the thing on. And they thought that Canada could do even better."

But first the group had to find a suitable site for such a prestigious event as the Winter Olympics.

Above: Although his postwar shipping business foundered, Franz never lost his passion for the B.C. coast.
Opposite: Summer in Symphony Bowl. From the moment he set foot in Whistler's high country, Franz knew he'd found his life's passion.

Franz (left) with Willy Schaeffler. To build the best ski area, Franz figured he'd have to consult with the best in the business.

SELF-PROPELLED IN GARIBALDI PROVINCIAL PARK

Photogenic and arresting. Garibaldi's Black Tusk.

I t was raining when we left. The clouds hung down over the valley like spider webs in a haunted house. Through the strands of mist, smears of green forest would emerge every now and then. Rainforest green. In the morning half-light, we'd catch sight of a distant peak. Then everything would disappear again. Except for the rain. It just kept coming down.

Our boots made squishing sounds in the slush. My brother kept looking at me with a quizzical look on his face. I don't think he really believed we were going skiing.

I couldn't blame him. The temperature was hovering just above freezing level, and the three feet of new snow that had fallen in the valley during the week was pockmarked and mushy from the rain. My pack already weighed heavily on my shoulders, and my skis dripped big droplets of cold water on my head. Did we really want to do this?

Sure, we did. Despite the warming trend, I had my heart set on climbing up into the protected snowfields just below the Black Tusk, that legendary hunk of basalt on the outskirts of Garibaldi Provincial Park. I knew it would be a long, wet climb to snow level. And I knew my brother wasn't particularly keen to follow. But I also knew how good the skiing would be once we got there.

Ah, British Columbia's Coast Mountains. Rising fully formed from the Pacific like a hydra-headed monster, its jumble of glaciated peaks and semi-dormant volcanoes has yet to be domesticated. Every season produces at least a couple of horror stories for the Vancouver media to dissect. "Woman goes for afternoon hike and disappears on mountain." "Lone snowshoer lost for five days." "Avalanche kills three skiers near Whistler." A trip into the Coast Mountains is like walking off the edge of the civilized world.

Besides, it's a land blessed by the gods. A place where steep, snow-crowned mountains thrust up precipitously from glacier-cut fjords. Where moisture-laden Pacific storms dump oodles of white stuff from October till May. A fun-hog's paradise. A place where you can ski powder in the morning, mountain bike or kayak at lunch, and sail on the ocean in the afternoon.

But the Coast Mountains are more than that, for they provide one of the few remaining connections to our primeval past. Despite the terrifying scars left by nearly a century's worth of logging, these mountains still nurture the last significant stands of old-growth temperate rainforest in the world. Ragged-bark cedars, monster Sitka spruce and majestic Douglas fir—trees that were already mature when explorer Simon Fraser first crossed the range in 1808— still stand proudly on mountain slopes and dark valley glades. These are forests whose tangled undergrowth could rival any Brazilian jungle for impassability. Brambles and salmonberry and devil's club tear at your clothes; climbing honeysuckle and blackberry and alder impede your passage at every turn. And wildlife. So much wildlife. Grizzlies and black bears, cougars, wildcats and wolverines still roam the highland valleys. Deer and mountain sheep and mountain goat and elk still graze the alpine meadows.

No exaggeration. While tens of thousands of vacationers clog the tortured arteries of nearby Whistler and Blackcomb each week of the winter, the mountains nearby are virtually devoid of human presence. And nowhere is that more evident than in Garibaldi Provincial Park. Created in 1920 and encompassing more than 480,000 acres of some of the most rugged—yet accessible— mountain wilderness in British Columbia, Garibaldi Park is also a haven for the self-propelled. While snowmobiles and helicopters are free to explore elsewhere in the Coast Mountains, the park is off-limits to all but hikers, climbers, snowshoers and skiers. Even mountain biking is forbidden within Garibaldi's boundaries. And that makes for some mighty fine backcountry touring.

But be forewarned! The Coast Mountains are not forgiving of mistakes. Touring in Garibaldi's high country requires careful preparation. And years of experience.

By the time we cleared the tree line, the storm had blown itself out. A fresh westerly wind was rising, and scraps of clouds bustled across the sky. Across the valley, a line of peaks extended as far as our eyes could see. To the west, the snow-pasted Tantalus range shimmered in the afternoon light. Directly above us was the great rock finger they call Black Tusk.

"Not a bad place," admitted my brother.

As we quickly changed into dry gear in the shelter of a last glade of scrubby spruce, I pointed out the line I wanted to take up the exposed ridge above us. The storm had left a thick blanket of white all around. Everything looked soft— incredibly inviting. And there was no one else around to share it with.

"What are we waiting for?" said my brother, after we'd dug a snow pit to evaluate the avalanche danger. Things looked good. Really good. By the time I'd hoisted my pack back onto my shoulders, he was already nearly a hundred yards ahead, breaking trail toward the ridge.

We spent the rest of the afternoon yo-yoing up and down the meadowed hills and gullies that surround Black Tusk. The snow was feathery soft and deep. And the skiing was mind-boggling. Bottomless powder. Face shots so intense we had to stop every now and then to clear off our goggles and catch our breaths.

"Good thing we didn't let the rain discourage us from coming up," I said during one of our breaks.

"What rain?" asked my brother.

Led by Sidney Dawes and Dave Mathews, the COA committee began by investigating the Diamondhead area around Squamish. "But I knew it wouldn't work there," said Wilhelmsen. "It just wasn't the right terrain for a world-class resort. A group of us had already been scouting around the same region with the idea of building a new ski area. So I talked them into going farther north, up the valley to Alta Lake and Whistler Mountain, which was then called London Mountain." He couldn't help but drop a chuckle. "And they were impressed."

The summer business in Alta Lake had been stagnating since the end of World War II. Customs had changed since Alex and Myrtle Philip had arrived 50 years before. People were now venturing further afield for their holidays. While the lakeside lodges still drew visitors (mostly older; mostly nostalgic for a past time), the area no longer carried the cachet it once did. Now logging ruled the valley. The proceeds from summer tourism were a distant second to the money rolling in from the sales of the rich first-growth timber extracted from the surrounding hills.

Still, despite all the industrial activity in the region, living conditions remained as rustic in the valley as they had been when Rainbow Lodge was built in 1915. The only way to get here was by train. There was no electricity, no running water and no telephone.

But Franz was already convinced this remote mountain valley had what it took for the development of a modern, new ski resort. He'd finally found his life's mission—the project he could stake his reputation on. "Subsequent to the visit by the COA, a group of businessmen from Vancouver got together and formed the Garibaldi Olympic Development Association—of which I was a member," said Wilhelmsen. "GODA's plan was to develop the south flank of Whistler Mountain—which are the slopes that drop into the Cheakamus side. But I wasn't convinced that was the right exposure for a new resort."

At the time, Franz was part of a group of young jet-setting Vancouverites—people like Chunky Woodward, Eric Beardmore and Peter Bentley—who regularly went on ski holidays to Europe. "We'd learned a lot from our trips to the Alps," Wilhelmsen explained. "We were all interested in building a new ski area around here because the local mountains were too short and too crowded. And we knew what we wanted. So when this Olympic push came around, we talked those people into coming and having a look at the other side of Whistler. But they weren't really interested."

Franz had experienced something of an epiphany on one of his climbs up the mountain that summer. During a multiday camping trip in the high-alpine region with a group of friends, Wilhelmsen got his first ever glimpse of Whistler Mountain's third—and most extensive—alpine bowl (what we call Glacier Bowl today). It became immediately apparent to Franz and his friends that this area was unlike anything they'd seen in the region to date: much bigger in scope, safer, with a greater variety of terrain and ideal exposure. "I realized right then and there just how spectacular the north side of Whistler was. I knew that's where we should build our lifts."

That's when Franz decided to take matters into his own hands. On November 21, 1960, he and a coterie of 10 friends launched their own private company, Garibaldi Lifts Limited. Franz was proclaimed president (a title he wouldn't relinquish for nearly 20 years). "We all put up some money between us in order to engage the finest consultant we could find. We were smart enough to realize that we didn't know the first thing about developing a ski area. We knew what we wanted. We just weren't sure how to get it." At the time, the best-known and most-respected ski area consultant in North America was Willy Schaeffler. "So that's who we got," explained Wilhelmsen.

Schaeffler traveled up to Alta Lake a number of times during 1961 and 1962. And he, too, was excited by Whistler's potential. The plan he finally drew up for Garibaldi Lifts Limited called for a north-side development on Whistler, with runs dropping down to the Fitzsimmons Creek drainage. "The plan," recalled Wilhelmsen, "was to build an all-weather road from the valley floor to a bench roughly 1,500 feet higher [about where the Express mid-load is situated today], where we'd build a village of chalets and condominiums. And it would have been an excellent development."

Unfortunately, the Fitzsimmons side of the mountain was riddled with mining claims. Although few claims were being worked at the time, the area had been extensively explored some decades before. "You just had to look at a mining claim map of the area—it was like a grid. Totally plastered with claims." And in British Columbia during the 1960s, mining claims (even dormant ones) took precedence over anything as dubious as plans for a new ski area. "So the government turned down our proposal."

But Wilhelmsen refused to give up. "Well," he recounted, "if they weren't going to let us develop the north side, we'd find another way up." So they invited Willy Schaeffler back up to Canada for another round of

A man and his mountain. When Whistler Mountain opened in 1966, it redefined the boundaries of the modern North American ski resort.

planning. "Fortunately for us, he wrote a very good feasibility report about the area we now call Creekside." And fortunately for them, there were no mining claims on that side of the mountain.

Schaeffler's report was, indeed, impressive.

"All my findings in the Whistler Mountain area in regard to a summer and winter recreation area are very encouraging: the high alpine character of the above-timberline area (the unparalleled magnificent view), the unlimited skiing potential above and below timberline for recreational skiing purposes, as well as for international competition requirements—the accessibility to a city of half a million by railroad, future highway and aircraft—the growth of skiing in general as a sport for the individual as well as for the family. It is everything the beginner, intermediate, advanced and expert skier could look for. At the same time, all the requirements for international ski competition are guaranteed in the most challenging terrain offered on this mountain."

For the next two years, Franz spent every second weekend tramping up the slopes of Whistler to record snow, wind and weather conditions. His only companion on most of these trips was a young Austrian mountaineer by the name of Stephan Ples. Only a few years before, Ples had bought a cabin in Alta Lake. He'd also started an alpine club and was completely devoted to the mountains around his new home. "If Franz represented the business side of the project," says a friend of both, "then Stephan represented the soul. He was never in it for the money. He just wanted to share his passions. Wanted to make sure that more people would have access to the mountains he loved."

Given the isolation of Whistler in those days, these weekend trips were an impressive undertaking. "We'd take the train up the night before and stay at the Hillcrest Lodge," said Franz. "We'd get up at 5:00 in the morning, hike all the way up to the top of the logging road, wait for daylight, then climb up through

the trees to timberline. At around 2:00, we'd ski back down to the valley with our data." That's 4,000 vertical feet of skiing, up and down, through untracked snow in coastal rainforest. It's an amazing feat even today, but an unbelievable accomplishment given the still-rudimentary ski gear Franz and Stephan were using in the early '60s. "Waiting for the train in the evening," remembered Franz, "I'd be so tired I didn't even know my name sometimes."

But they kept doing it. In summer as well as winter. In good weather and in bad. "We sure got into good shape," admitted Franz. "And we sure got to know our mountain."

Now more than ever, Franz was determined to get this project off the ground and flying.

All Garibaldi Lifts Limited needed now was money. "That's when we decided to go to the public to raise the required funds. We already had an agreement with the B.C. government that they would set aside a 56-acre plot at the base of the mountain for us to buy if we performed to their satisfaction. They also agreed to push the highway up from Squamish to Whistler if we raised enough money to prove that we could really develop this thing."

So the company started selling shares. But not in a conventional way. "Normally you go to an underwriter or a broker and they raise the money for you for a fee. But the brokers in Vancouver didn't take us seriously. They laughed when we presented our prospectus. They didn't want to have anything to do with us."

With few alternatives to fall back on, the company's board of directors decided to sell the shares themselves. They gave themselves two years to raise $800,000. And they added a few creative wrinkles to their offering.

"All the money that was raised from the public went into a trust," explained Franz. "And the money wouldn't be released to the company until three conditions had been met: [1] we had to reach at least a total subscription of $450,000 (to ensure we had enough to complete the project); [2] the highway had to be built to the parking lot; and [3] we had to secure government agreement for the leases, easement and forestry clearing for the base area.

If we failed these conditions, then the trust company would pay back the money to the investors—with interest. We thought it was such a safe investment, it couldn't lose. I mean, we even offered shares on the installment plan. And a half-price discount on season's passes for any shareholder for five years."

A prospectus was produced and 5,000 copies were dis-

Waiting for the gondola, 1970.
Liftlines during Whistler's early
days could be daunting.

Ski racing has been a part of Whistler Mountain since its very inception.

Some people still blame Montreal for Whistler's failed 1976 Olympic bid. "We had everything going our way," they'll argue. "A great committee. A wonderful location. An amazing plan. And virtually no competition. If Montreal hadn't been the frontrunner to host the Summer Games in '76 we would have surely hosted the Winter Games here on the West Coast instead."

If only...

Born on the wings of an Olympic dream, Whistler has always had something of an obsession with this great international sports festival. Even today, when one might be excused for thinking that it has all the accolades it needs, Whistler's Olympic thirst is still not slaked. A serious candidate for the 2010 Winter Games, Vancouver/Whistler is fighting hard for recognition as the bid city of choice. In fact, millions of dollars are being spent right now on trying to convince the winter-sports world to come to British Columbia at the end of the decade for the quadrennial celebrations. "It would be an incredible achievement for all Canadians," says the irrepressible Nancy Greene-Raine, herself an Olympic gold medalist in 1968. "Hosting the Games is a once-in-a-lifetime opportunity. And it's not to be taken lightly. It's something you'll be telling your kids and your grandkids about for years to come."

Indeed. And the thirst for the Games has never been stronger around here. Whistler has been trying to host the Olympics now for over 40 years. From the moment in 1960 when Canada's International Olympic Committee member, Sidney Dawes, endorsed the Whistler area as a potential site for a future Winter Games, there has always been a surprisingly strong current of support for the high-stakes poker playing required to land the Olympics here. No matter what the cost. No matter what the consequences.

And though they tried for the 1972 Games, and again in 1980, it was the 1976 bid that definitely came the closest to winning all the marbles. "Only when we have traveled the lonely and surprisingly vast distance to the limits of our own courage will we discover new frontiers," stated the introduction to the official Vancouver/Garibaldi bid book. "The young of all nations are invited to begin a second journey of exploration in the new world in 1976."

The year was 1968. Whistler had been in operation for barely two seasons. But already, the Canadian Olympic Association was impressed enough with its physical plant to endorse the region's bid to host the Games of the XII Winter Olympiad as the official Canadian entry (only one site per country is allowed in the "game"). And what a different place Whistler would have become had it won that bid!

Not surprisingly (given the limited scope of the development on site at the time), the '76 Games proposal called for a complete redesign of the facilities on Whistler Mountain. Rather than being developed in the original Creekside area at the south end of the valley—or even at the future Whistler Village site on the north side—the proposed 8,000-bed Olympic town was to be located on the shores of Alta Lake, roughly halfway between the two sites. While most of the facilities (stadium, media center, etc.) would be on the mountain side of Highway 99, the athletes' accommodations would all be on the lake side. Adjacent to the new town (and accessible by foot) would be a brand-new train station to greet guests and competitors arriving daily by rail.

In keeping with the times, the architects' drawings of the new town site were ultramodern in conception. Everything was sharp angles, glass and steel. There was little in the architectural plans, in fact, that reflected anything of a West-Coast flavor. Nothing that built on an alpine tradition, even. Still, the thought of a mountain village with a lakefront development on one side and a ski hill on the other leads to all kinds of "what-ifs?"

And the whole thing was still based on a pedestrian-friendly concept. All the venues, asserted the proposal, would be within a two-and-a-half-mile radius of the new Olympic town site. Four new lifts were proposed for the northwest side of Whistler Mountain and a state-of-the-art nordic facility was planned for the undulating terrain at the base of Blackcomb Mountain now called The Benchlands. A heliport, a hospital, a speed-skating oval, a hockey stadium: they were all there.

It was an impressive proposal. And it came very close to winning the competition. Unfortunately for Whistler, the lobbyists for the Denver committee had more clout with International Olympic Committee voters and the bid went south.

In an ironic twist that few in Vancouver or Whistler could really appreciate, Denver was the first city in Olympic history whose citizens eventually voted to reject the honor of hosting the Games. Innsbruck, Austria, agreed in the 11th hour to stand in as an alternative site.

Whistler Peak after a storm.
What's not to like?

tributed to the public. But Vancouver investors were still leery and very slow to jump on the Whistler bandwagon.

"It took us the whole two years to raise those funds," said Franz. "And we had to twist some arms pretty seriously to get there. But finally we were ready to proceed."

With the road well on its way to Whistler, Franz and his team started the Herculean task of setting up the construction site for work. "Alta Lake was still very much a wilderness area," he said. "There were still no facilities whatsoever that we could harness. But we were determined to proceed. In May of 1964, we went and delivered two tractors and a crew of men to the base of the mountain. And all they did for the next two months was clear the present-day Creekside parking lot—which was going to be the camp for the workers who would build the lifts."

Over the next two years, the southwest side of Whistler Mountain would become a hive of activity. And Garibaldi Lifts Limited would continue to break new ground. The company also exploited any assets its directors might have at hand—like those of Glen McPherson, for example, the president of Okanagan Helicopters. "We were the first in the country to pour concrete for our lift tower placements by helicopter," a proud Wilhelmsen

explained. "It was Glen who made that possible for us. We used aluminum beer barrels, which we filled up with concrete in the valley and flew up to the sites. It was an impressive sight in those days, I can tell you."

As could be expected in such a wild setting, there were setbacks. A union dispute shut the site down for a while. As did a number of forest-fire closures.

It wasn't easy. And it wasn't always fun. But by the end of 1965, a four-passenger gondola, a double chairlift and two T-bars were in place. A half-dozen runs were cut, and a base lodge, a gondola barn, a midmountain lift station and a summit warming hut (which doubled as a base for the ski patrol team) were all built. On New Year's Day, 1966, the residents of Alta Lake were treated to a free ride up the mountain. Six weeks later, on February 15, 1966, Whistler Mountain officially opened its doors to the public.

Everyone was impressed. Franz Wilhelmsen was even proclaimed "Man of the Year" by the Greater Vancouver Tourist Bureau. But his travails were far from over.

"We still had to deal with the Hydro company," he said. "When we told them how many people would be living here in the future—how many thousands of watts we'd need in two or three years—they just

Above: An enthusiastic booster in the early days—and a keen skier himself—Canadian icon Pierre Elliot Trudeau spent part of his honeymoon on Whistler Mountain.
Opposite: Whistler Mountain's Bagel Bowl. Snow-pasted trees, a rising mist and a late-afternoon run down to meet the sun.

FRANZ' RUN

THIS SKI RUN, WITH THE GREATEST VERTICAL FALL IN NORTH AMERICA,
IS DEDICATED TO
FRANZ M. WILHELMSEN
ONE OF THE FOUNDERS OF THE WHISTLER DEVELOPMENT AND PRESIDENT,
FROM 1960 TO 1983, OF THE WHISTLER MOUNTAIN SKI CORPORATION AND
OF ITS PREDECESSOR., GARIBALDI LIFTS LTD.

THIS DEDICATION IS MADE IN APPRECIATION
OF HIS VISIONARY FORESIGHT AND HIS WILL
TO DEVELOP A SKI AREA EQUAL TO NONE, BY THE
OWNERS, MANAGEMENT AND STAFF OF THE
WHISTLER MOUNTAIN SKI CORPORATION.
DECEMBER 10, 1983

laughed in our face. 'You're never gonna get power in there, because you're never going to need all that power,' they told us. After all, they were used to being approached by people full of dreams. And for the most part, their dreams amounted to little. But we pushed and pushed and they finally let up."

The compromise offered by B.C. Hydro was not much more than a band-aid solution to Whistler's energy woes, however. By the fall of 1968, the situation was getting serious. "They still didn't really believe in us at that point. Still—they finally brought in this diesel electric station on the train. And it was housed in a railway car. Well—it wasn't long before there was a second railway car there. And by Christmas time, there was a third one sitting alongside the other two."

But to work properly, a diesel electric station has to stay fueled up. "During Christmas week, the Hydro caretaker got drunk, passed out in his cabin and they all ran out of fuel. So the machines stopped. And the whole valley froze up." Indeed, that power failure, coupled with extremely low temperatures for the following five days, resulted in closure of the lifts and a complete evacuation of the valley. "It cost us a lot of money," remem-

bered Franz. "It took us nearly a month and a half to get the valley back in operation." He smiled. "That's when B.C. Hydro decided to put a proper substation in."

Still—despite the setbacks, despite the weather challenges, despite the skeptics even—Whistler Mountain continued to grow. "No matter what anybody says today," Franz told me in 1986, during the company's 20-year celebration, "there wasn't one of us back in 1966 who could have predicted how big this place would eventually become. In 1962, we set out to build a major new ski area for the enjoyment of the population of the Lower Mainland. And we did that—very well. The rest of it—Blackcomb and the town center, and all the fancy new hotels and restaurants and destination tourists—well, I for one, could have never envisioned it."

On Thursday, April 30, 1998, Franz Wilhelmsen—hailed around the world as Whistler's Founding Father—passed away in Vancouver. "I will always think of him as one of the most valuable mentors in my career," says Hugh Smythe, the president of Intrawest's Resort Operations Group. "Franz was incredibly perceptive, had a great sense of humor and was charming and gentlemanly in every situation."

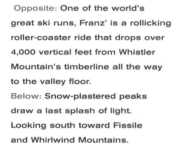

Opposite: **One of the world's great ski runs, Franz' is a rollicking roller-coaster ride that drops over 4,000 vertical feet from Whistler Mountain's timberline all the way to the valley floor.**
Below: **Snow-plastered peaks draw a last splash of light. Looking south toward Fissile and Whirlwind Mountains.**

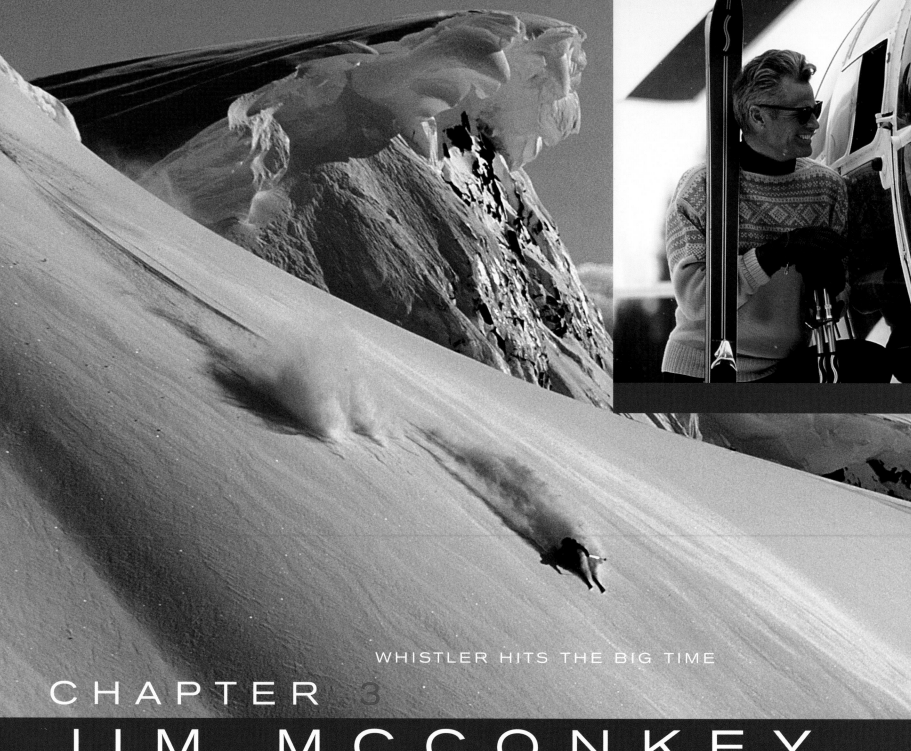

CHAPTER 3

JIM MCCONKEY

Back in the early '70s, Whistler was still very much on the edge of the world—an unknown ski area lost in the

wild Coast Range of British Columbia. It had a base lodge, a gas station, a couple of hotels and three restaurants

to choose from (if they were all open at the same time). There were no tourists to speak of.

For dedicated ski bums, it was a dream come true. Except for weekends—when Vancouverites would descend

on the area in hordes—the place was empty. The mountain was ours. All 5,000 vertical feet of it. Being a ski

instructor there was easy. Lacking for students on most days, we were free to ski to our heart's content.

Fortunately, we had a boss who assumed that we were all at Whistler for the same reason. In fact, he was the

one who most often led the downhill charge. And he led it with verve. To us rookie pros, Jim McConkey was definitely bigger than life. He was Diamond Jim. He was The Master.

One of the great all-terrain skiers in history, McConkey, now 76, is better known today as the father of that other great all-terrain skier, Shane McConkey. But back when I first met him in 1974, Diamond Jim was a major talent.

He was the man whose smooth-skiing style and mind-bending jumps had come to embody the great technical leaps of the '50s and '60s. He was a skier whose name was synonymous with big-mountain adventures, a guy who had appeared in almost every major ski movie made in America over the past two decades.

I still remember my first day on the job at Whistler. It was puking snow the way it does only in the Pacific Northwest, straight down and thick as molasses. I'd spent the night shivering on a friend's floor in an unheated cabin and felt like old dog food. I was definitely not ready to spend the next two hours babysitting tourists on a mountain I barely knew.

Luckily, there were no clients at the ski-school bell that morning. In what I would come to know as typical

McConkey style, the boss didn't even wait around for potential clients who might straggle in a little late. On the stroke of 10, he gave us our marching orders.

"Hey Michel, Finn, Fuji. Grab your skis. We're going up to Insanity."

Insanity?

I didn't have a clue what Insanity was. But I was game for anything. I was on the West Coast. I was living and working in the mountains. I was in paradise.

By the time we disembarked from the gondola at midstation, the snow was coming down even harder. Visibility was just past nil. Probably three feet of fresh stuff lay on the ground—thick and pasty and hard to walk through. "Okay, you guys," instructed Jim, "Straight down the fall line. High-speed turns. And remember—let 'em run, or you'll get bogged down."

That was it. He stepped into his bindings and pushed off down the hill, heading straight for the upper gondola tower and what appeared to be a sizeable cliff band below. All I could see beyond that were tight, little stands of second-growth evergreens interspersed with more cliffs and more towers. This was not a run. This wasn't even an approximation of a run. This was Insanity. I decided to stick close to the boss.

Opposite: Talented, fearless and always up for an adventure, McConkey broke new ground every time he stepped in his skis. Here he jumps a plane in the Bugaboos in the 1960s.
Below: Even today, Whistler skiers continue to push the boundaries.

I listen to the telephone message a second time, just to make sure. "Hey Mich," says the slightly manic voice of photographer Eric Berger. "Drop what you're doin' right now and listen. We're goin' ridin' tomorrow. Brian Savard is coming. Dano Pendygrasse, too. It's gonna be great. We're meeting in the Mountain Heli-Sport parking lot at 7:00. No excuses. Just be there!"

And then a click.

I shake my head in wonder.

Spring has already come and gone. Whistler and Blackcomb are both closed for the season, and the glacier lifts don't open for another week. For most valley denizens, the focus shifted long ago from riding and skiing to mountain biking and climbing.

But not for us snow junkies. So what if it's summer in the valley. So what if the commercial heli-skiing season is long past. We've got a bird and a guide and we're goin' flying. And in our own backyard.

At first I'm skeptical. The weather at the Whistler heliport looks far from promising. Great big rolling cumuli are building darkly above our heads. It looks even meaner up north. The pilot shakes his head.

"You still want to go up?" he asks. Aside from our little party, the heliport is deserted.

"Why not?" says Eric. "We're here. We're keen. Let's go."

"It's your trip," says the pilot.

Suddenly we're airborne, the A-Star eating up vertical effortlessly over a bluff and into the next valley. Below us an old logging road runs along a meandering river. Classic moose territory. Long streamers of mist start to interpose themselves between us and the ground. Rain appears on the windshield.

We come squirming through a thick, cloudy soup of pelting snow and rain into bright summer sunshine. The helicopter strains a little against the fresh westerly that comes singing over the high col. My heart begins to pound faster. Our guide, Mike McCall, grabs my elbow and points to a series of snow-pasted peaks to my left. Clouds rise up around them and dissipate as quickly as they're formed. "That's where we're going," he says into the microphone. "Looks almost clear enough to land, too."

I nod. A silly grin starts to spread across my face. There are daffodils growing in Vancouver, the cherry trees have already flowered, and I'm up in a helicopter getting ready to drop into some serious riding terrain where granite and snow dominate. And more snow. Nearly 25 feet of the stuff, McCall estimates.

McCall guides the pilot down to our landing site, and the four of us tumble out—into thigh-deep powder.

"Baby," exclaims a surprised Berger. "This is a lot softer than I expected." At least six inches of the soft stuff is new from last night. Summer powder, for sure!

The helicopter disappears in a whine of blades and motor. Then silence. For a moment nobody talks. A monster raven rides an uprising valley thermal.

We're standing on a steep ridge at about 8,000 feet of altitude. Above our heads loom a trio of unnamed peaks with sickly steep rocky faces (and perfect little shots between the rocks for some highly stylized hero moves). Below us is a vertical sea of white, mostly wide-open, high-speed choogling terrain.

"What are we waiting for?" asks McCall. And he pushes off into the fall line.

Local hero Savard points his snowboard downhill and takes off in hot pursuit. Fast. Really fast. He's halfway down the slope already, appearing to barely touch the surface of the snow from turn to turn. Up a little side ridge and then a big, loopy jump off the lip. Sticks it cleanly and is back for more.

I don't wait for an invitation. By the first turn, I know I'm into something special. The snow is soft and silky, yet firm and bouncy, too. And the visibility is improving by the minute. Turning is effortless.

And then—too soon—the run is over. Three thousand vertical feet covered in a couple of dozen turns. What a rush. What a way to greet the summer.

Whistler freerider Brian Savard rips it up in the backcountry.

Long before his son Shane ever posed for a camera, McConk was a film star in his own right. Here he is with Sally Neidlinger in *Ski Crazy*.

Now Jim was no youngster. He was nearing 50, and his hair had long turned to silver. Sure he was a legend and everything. But the guy was old.

I, on the other hand, hadn't even seen 20 yet and was as fit as I would ever be in my life. I figured it would be no problem keeping up to the old guy. I was wrong.

Halfway down Insanity, I began to struggle. My goggles were fogging up, my heart was pounding and my legs were already beginning to lose their spring. Clearly, this deep Whistler stuff was a whole new world. I had snow in my mouth, in my ears and down my parka. I could barely see or breathe, let alone concentrate on my line.

Jim, on the other hand, was still dancing. He was three or four turns ahead of me and seemed to float effortlessly over the heavy snow. And that pissed me off. Legend or not, there was no way I was going to let this guy get away from me. I straightened my line in a desperate attempt to close the gap. I could see the bottom of the run. I figured I had enough juice to pass him. Wrong again.

Just as I caught up with him, Jim made a big sweeping turn to the right and disappeared from sight. Suddenly I understood. Ahead of me was nothing. Picture the wild contortions of a cat in mid air. Or the antics of Wile E. Coyote as he desperately tries to avoid another crash. That was me in mid turn, sailing over the 20-foot cliff that Jim had so neatly avoided.

Bang. Welcome to Whistler. Bang. Welcome to big-mountain skiing. Bang. Welcome to your new job. And then nothing.

My boss was the first to reach me. He arrived just as I was able to free my right hand and frantically clear enough snow from my face to get in a sobbing breath. My left arm was broken where I'd landed on it, my shoulder was badly bruised and I had dislocated my baby finger. I was trying not to blubber out loud.

"Nice jump, Michel," boomed McConkey, a huge grin on his face, as he helped dig me out of my landing crater. "Good leap." He laughed, dusting some of the snow off my back. "But around here, we don't count 'em if you don't ski out of 'em."

And that was the last I heard about it. I skied the rest of the season with a badly damaged arm and a much greater appreciation for the complexities of big-mountain skiing. Oh, yeah—and I never tried to pass McConkey again on a run I didn't know.

"That was a wonderful time of my life," says McConkey with a twinkle in his eye. "I loved skiing so much in those days. I just wanted to share my passion with others. Teach them how to ski in all conditions so they could enjoy the sport as much as I did. And I think it worked."

Indeed. Now retired, the still-very-active septuagenarian spends half the year puttering around his island retreat on B.C.'s Georgia Strait and the other half playing golf with his old ski cronies in Southern California. He still skis from time to time. Hunts a lot, too. And he still exudes that special *joie de vivre* that was so much his trademark during his tenure as Whistler's first bona fide ski ambassador.

"He definitely set a high standard during those years," says Tom Ladner, one of Whistler Mountain's early directors. "He had a way of skiing—and teaching—that got everyone enthused. No matter the conditions—and they could get pretty tough at Whistler in those days—skiing with Jim was always fun."

While most of today's skiers get their start in formal ski schools or high-tech racing programs, McConkey got his in the wilds of eastern Canada. At age 12, he would regularly set out into the forests around his home in Barrie, Ontario, with a .22-caliber rifle on his back and a pair of skis on his feet.

"It was the Depression," he explains, "and fresh game was always welcome." He laughs, still the booming, confident laugh that I remember so well. "But really, that was just a front. We didn't really need the meat I brought home. It was just my excuse to get out for an adventure in the backcountry. I lived for the outdoors back then. I lived for the moment when I would strap on my skis and push off into the unknown."

Not surprisingly, the rolling hills of eastern Canada couldn't hope to hold his attention for long. By the summer of 1948, Jim had crossed the country and was living and working in Banff, Alberta. But it was an invitation to join Alf Engen's ski school at Utah's Alta in 1953 that really set him on his path.

Although powder skiing was still in its infancy back then, Alta, with its light snow and steep slopes, was quickly earning a reputation as the place to be for powder aficionados. There, ski school director Engen had assembled a team of talented instructors that included Junior Bounous ("Probably the best all-round skier I've ever had the opportunity to ski with," says McConkey), Ted Johnson (who would go on to develop Snowbird), Olympic medalist Franz Gabl and famed avalanche expert Ed LaChapelle. "We had so much fun during those years," says McConkey. "There was just a handful

McConk did more than anyone to popularize Whistler's unrivaled glade skiing. He called it "Whistler's secret weapon."

of us who were proficient at skiing in deep-snow conditions. So we ended up teaching a lot of lessons. And getting loads of publicity." He laughs again. "I guess, in a way, we were the powder-skiing kings of that era."

Technology had yet to make a big impact on the ski business. Skiing was still a sport that was based on athletic prowess more than on hardware. And McConkey and his gang had athletic talent to spare. "We were still skiing on 220-cm skis, remember. Boards that were stiff as heck with virtually no sidecut and near-impossible to turn. As for the boots, forget about it. We got more support from the longthong straps that we wrapped around our ankles than the boots themselves."

Which makes those classic Alta powder shots from that era even more impressive. "It was a truly inspiring group of people to hang out with," says McConkey. "We used to meet for last ride of the day—a whole gang of us. We'd pick a line or an off-piste run we wanted to do, and head out together. Most days, we wouldn't make it back until well after dark."

Photos from that time show a youthful McConkey flying off impossibly tall cliffs, always in perfect position over his skis, or making big snowboard-like turns in deep, untracked snow. And smooth, always so smooth. "We didn't consider what we were doing 'extreme,'" he says. "We were just out to have a good time."

McConkey spent 10 years at Alta. "Maybe the best years of my life," he says. "We lived a subsistence existence back then. But we truly loved what we were doing. We were utterly committed to the experience."

Experience was fine, but a fellow had to make a living, too. And McConkey had a definite plan. "Franz Wilhelmsen and Eric Beardmore used to come down to Alta and stay at the Rustler Lodge," he remembers. "At the time, I was looking for a situation where I could run a ski school and a ski shop on a franchise basis. This new project of theirs at

Whistler Mountain looked darned interesting."

Whistler would have to wait, however. First, McConkey took a job directing the new ski school at Park City, Utah. "But I was on a salary there," he says, "and that's not what I wanted." In a gutsy move, Jim decided to move back to Canada and start a school at Tod Mountain (now Sun Peaks) deep in the interior of B.C. "I spent four winters there. I pioneered the place. But the ski school just wasn't happening. There was no beginner area, no real teaching situation."

Meanwhile, Wilhelmsen and his cohorts had managed to get Whistler up and running. And it was beginning to turn heads. "Right from the beginning, I had my eye on Whistler," explains McConkey. "And the reasons were simple. Skiing had developed enough by the mid '60s that the kids who were coming up would want a more challenging mountain. And Whistler definitely provided a good challenge. I was also looking for a resort where the season was really long. I wasn't a carpenter or a builder—didn't have any summer trade to tide me over—so I wanted a ski shop that didn't close its doors for six months of the year. Whistler fit my requirements perfectly."

And McConkey's lofty stature in the skiing world seemed to fit Whistler's needs as well. "The arrangements we had in place were not working out, and we badly wanted to find a high-profile director for our school," Franz Wilhelmsen said in a 1977 interview. "So in the spring of 1968, I sent [mountain manager] Jack Bright and [patrol director] Hugh Smythe to Tod Mountain to see if we could entice Jim to Whistler."

It seemed like an ideal match, especially when Jim floated his franchise proposal. "I wasn't sure if they were going to buy it," admits McConkey. "But Franz being Franz, he really like the idea—especially the fact that I would be paying him, not him paying me."

But Whistler in the late '60s was still far from becoming the destination resort it is today. In fact, there really wasn't much there at all, except for a big mountain with a lot of snow. "When I first arrived at Whistler in April of 1968, there were only 20 names in the telephone book," remembers McConkey. "There were probably six kids—no more—in the school on the other side of the lake. If you needed groceries or had banking to do, you had to travel 30 miles down-valley to Squamish. And even there, you couldn't get much more than the basics."

McConkey wasn't worried, however. "I knew in my heart that Whistler was going to be a winner," he explains. "It was near a big city, with an international

Hiking high above the clouds
on Blackcomb Peak.

airport, and the road access to it wasn't all that bad—even though everyone complained about it."

Besides, the skiing was like nothing Jim had experienced before.

"My first year at Whistler, there was so much snow, it was hard to believe," he recalls. "It was fabulous skiing. There weren't any crowds midweek, and the mountain was still virtually unexplored. We had a great time."

Still, these were not easy times for anyone investing in the new resort. And Jim was no exception. "Those first few years were really tough," he admits. "Power failures, snow droughts, bridges collapsing—it seemed like the calamities never stopped."

His very first season in operation—the '68–'69 winter—seemed to set the tone for the next few years. "That first year, I gambled everything I had on building a new ski shop and setting myself up in business at the base of the mountain. Things started really well, and it looked for a while like my gamble was going to pay off handsomely. But during Christmas week, we had this huge power failure, followed by a massive freeze, and the resort had to shut down for a month and a half! I lost pretty much everything I had invested."

But the skiing was good and the people were fun. So Jim decided to stick it out and see what would happen. "To tell you the truth, I really enjoyed those years. Really loved it. I worked hard—no question about that—but getting up in the morning to go to work was never a chore. And I think those feelings were reflected in the personnel who worked for me. People loved to come down to the shop, hang out and talk about skiing."

The Whistler community was a small one in those years, and McConkey's house became something of a hangout for many of us. But Jim never seemed to mind. "I would put on regular parties at my house—with beer and wine and food—for my instructors, you know. And all the ski bums in the valley would show up for the free feed. But I didn't mind, really. I just loved what I was doing. And I guess people were attracted to that."

By 1970, Whistler had earned a reputation among young athletic skiers for its long powder slopes and uncrowded conditions. From Quebec to California, the word was out: Whistler was a happening place, and still relatively inexpensive. "You could get a day ticket for around $6 then," remembers Jim. "It was pretty cheap. But it was still too much for some of the young locals in the valley. I remember one year, Franz came up with the

Above: The skis are fatter. The boots are stiffer. And the bindings are way safer than they were in McConk's heyday. But the spirit remains the same. Getting first tracks is what it's all about. Opposite: Even as a silver-haired senior, McConk still charged harder—and skied faster—than pros half his age.

idea that if you hiked up to midstation, you could then ski for free. I don't think he believed that anyone would take him up on his offer. But he was wrong. That winter, every ski bum in the valley hiked to midstation."

Needless to say, that program was quickly retired.

Over the next two decades, McConkey would become one of the most recognized, and loved, figures on the mountain. A born proselytizer, he did more to promote skiing in B.C. than just about anybody else in the business. "It was a great time to be at Whistler," he says. "There I'd be, with a coffee cup in my hand, hanging out by the base lift, talking to people. I just loved it."

Jim wasn't just talking though. He was also breaking new ground in adventure skiing. "Glen McPherson had introduced helicopter service to Whistler Mountain very early on in its development," he remembers. "And they'd been offering sight-seeing tours around the local mountains for some time before I arrived." When McPherson retired as president of Okanagan Helicopters, his successor, John Pitts, approached McConkey to see if he'd be interested in running a heli-skiing operation from the top of Whistler Mountain.

"I thought it would be an excellent promotion for Whistler," says McConkey. "So I immediately accepted.

At the time—and for some years after—we were the only ski area in North America to provide heli-skiing on-site."

The region immediately surrounding Whistler is an adventure-skier's dream come true. Lofty peaks, massive glaciers, huge powder-filled bowls: It just doesn't get much better than this—anywhere. With a helicopter at your disposal to reach some of the more inaccessible slopes, Whistler suddenly becomes a playground both immeasurably vast and hugely entertaining.

Not surprisingly, Jim was at his best when he was in the mountains guiding clients. He was always up, always patient—and always ready with an encouraging word for his often-struggling guests. Didn't matter if it was the prime minister of Canada or the guy from down the street, Jim treated them all like old friends.

"It wasn't easy for skiers in those years," he explains. "Especially not with the kind of conditions we get around Whistler. Now with all those shaped skis and fat skis and such, it takes very little effort to ski powder. That wasn't always the case in the '60s and '70s."

As exciting as it was, as sexy as it appeared, flying in a helicopter was no big deal to Jim. It was simply a means to an end. "Skiing, for me, is a lot more than making turns on the side of a mountain," he says. "It's

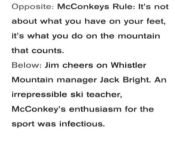

Opposite: **McConkeys Rule: It's not about what you have on your feet, it's what you do on the mountain that counts.**
Below: **Jim cheers on Whistler Mountain manager Jack Bright. An irrepressible ski teacher, McConkey's enthusiasm for the sport was infectious.**

about freedom and poetry and celebrating your passions with other like-minded people. It's about taking chances and learning about yourself. Learning who your real pals are. I always say: One of the best things about my ski career are the friends I've met along the way."

And he means it. "The guy has such soul," says longtime pro patroller Cathy Jewett. "When I broke my leg in the late '70s, Jim gave me a jacket that had been autographed by the man who skied down Everest. He thought that it would motivate me to heal faster. And you know what? It did."

McConkey ran the Whistler heli-skiing operation for seven years before turning it over to Herb Blauer, a professional guide and keen mountaineer. "It was a shame to let it go," says McConkey, "but the Whistler board of directors was getting increasingly concerned about liability. They were right to be nervous, of course. Still, it was one heck of a promotion for Whistler."

But Whistler had turned the corner by then. "I think the Whistler heli-skiing program was a good way to get our name out in the public eye. But there were a lot of other things happening on the mountain, too. The Toni Sailer Summer Camps, for example, had a huge impact on Whistler's future." Co-hosted by the three-time

Olympic gold medalist from Austria and Canada's own Olympic golden girl, Nancy Greene-Raine, the summer camps were hugely successful ventures—attracting young skiers from all over the world to the glaciated upper slopes of Whistler for weeklong skiing sessions in June and July. "To have people of Toni and Nancy's stature fronting the camp was a great coup for Whistler," says Jim.

Could he have ever imagined how big Whistler was going to get in those early years? "I don't think anybody could have," he admits. "We all knew it was a great place. And some of us realized how much potential it had. But to envision the kind of place Whistler has become would have taken far more foresight than I had at the time."

Jim McConkey was inducted into the Canadian Ski Hall of Fame in the fall of 2001. It was an honor long overdue. But Jim doesn't see it that way. "I was lucky to lead the life I did," he maintains. "And I still feel very fortunate to have my health and be surrounded by good friends and play golf every day and go hunting whenever I want to. True, we broke a lot of new ground at Whistler. There weren't many boundaries in those days. But there were no guarantees, neither. You just had to go out there and create a life for yourself that you were comfortable with. So that's what I did. And I have absolutely no regrets."

Above: **McConkey (far right) and teammates share the runner-up trophy in the legendary Snow, Earth, Water race in 1977. McConkey was always a fast skier and a canny racer.**
Opposite: **McConkey pioneered ski routes at Whistler that are still considered big adventures today.**

CHAPTER 4

HUGH SMYTHE

He was barely out of high school when he first moved up to Whistler—young and keen and raring to go. And he

knew exactly what he wanted to do on the mountain. "I already had a few years experience as a volunteer ski

patroller at Mt. Baker," says Hugh Smythe, who grew up in the Vancouver suburb of New Westminster. "But now

I wanted to become a pro. So I moved into Whistler's first aid room and worked for meals. By February, I was

finally working as a full-time patroller. It was like a dream come true."

The year was 1966. And unbeknownst to him, Hugh was about to embark on one of the greatest adventures

in modern ski-resort history. "I loved skiing," he says. "And I loved the mountains. That's all that mattered to me

during those first years. That's all I cared about."

Today, the 54-year-old Whistlerite is president of Intrawest's vast Resort Operations Group, a half-billion-dollar mountain empire that stretches across North America (and includes some of the most successful resorts in the world). He's also considered one of the most creative—and canny—operators in the resort business. And who can argue with that?

After all, it was Smythe, back in 1980, who launched Blackcomb Mountain, based on a new "total experience" philosophy, and then raised the bar for everyone in North America five years later by pushing a ski lift high into the resort's alpine region. It was Smythe again, in 1986, who convinced a Young Presidents Organization colleague, Joe Houssian, to invest in his Blackcomb dream, and then stunned the ski world, again, with a high-speed-lift network that raised the bar higher yet. It was Smythe, once more, in 1996, who managed to harness the power of two mountain rivals—Whistler and Blackcomb—and meld them into the industry-leading resort they've become today.

But make no mistake—Smythe is definitely not just another resort bean counter. While he may spend the majority of his working hours transiting in airport lounges or sitting in airless conference rooms checking facts and figures with his Intrawest colleagues, his first love is still the mountains. And he'll throw on a pair of skis and make some turns whenever his schedule allows him to. Tall, slightly stooped and sporting a full head of gray hair, he can often be found between corporate meetings flying down his favorite runs at Blackcomb or Whistler.

His skiing style is old school: feet close together, hands in front, upper body barely moving from turn to turn. Elegant. Classy. And always in control. "I still get the same rush from skiing as I did when I was a kid," he told me recently after a record nine-days-in-a-row stint on the mountain. "Maybe even more, given how good the new shaped skis have become. The only difference now is that I appreciate it like I never did in the past."

Smythe could live just about anywhere he wants to in North America. But he feels strongly that his family is best served by staying put at Whistler. "What more could you want for your kids?" he asks rhetorically. His delivery is machine-gun fast. His gaze is direct; his expression, guileless. "The schools are great. The environment is healthy. And the community is really strong. When I stop and think about it, what this community

Above: A relaxed Hugh Smythe, second from right, with the Whistler pro patrol in 1967. Hugh's strength as a mountain manager came from his working experience "on the line." Opposite: Whistler's Glacier Bowl from above the Roundhouse. In the early days, Whistler Mountain's alpine terrain was the ski patrol's private kingdom.

has achieved in the last 30 years is pretty amazing. And it all has to do with the can-do attitude of the people who first moved here." He smiles. "Sometimes I'm bowled over when I consider the confluence of talented people in this valley in the mid 1970s. To me, that's a huge part of the Whistler story."

Something of a traditionalist, Smythe has resisted all efforts to move him out of the corner office he's occupied in Blackcomb's administrative building since it was built in 1986. In fact, when Intrawest designed a whole suite of fancy offices for its senior operations staff a few years back, Smythe was the only holdout. "I guess I'm kind of like the little old guy who built his corner grocery store into a national concern," he explains. "When I look out my office window, I still get to see our guests boarding the lifts. And for some reason, that's a thrilling sight to me. It reminds me every day what we are all about."

He's also a bit of a micromanager and never hesitates to take matters into his own hands and change things if he thinks he can improve them. And while that trait has driven some of his employees to distraction, it also ensures a level of excellence at his resorts that has become legendary in the business.

"Hugh," says longtime friend and former colleague

Roger McCarthy, "has an amazing ability to pinpoint exactly what would make an experience, any experience, magical for the guest—be it skiing with your family, strolling around the shops, lunch with friends or hitting the nightspots. He has this unbridled passion about everything that he does, in his work and in his personal life, and he really believes in making things fun."

Consider his groundbreaking work in big-mountain safety, for example. "It was definitely pioneering stuff," Hugh admits of his early pro patrol years at Whistler Mountain. "Mostly, we were making it up as we went along. Remember, there were virtually no cut runs at first on Whistler. And even the runs we did have were rough beyond modern skiers' understanding. Making the mountain safe for people back then was definitely a different kind of job than it is today."

Even more treacherous than the state of its slopes, however, was the ever-looming threat of avalanches. With the number of skiers visiting Whistler steadily rising every year—and venturing farther afield—it was soon apparent that the patrol would have to play a much more aggressive role in the management of its high-alpine slopes.

And it would be up to people like Smythe, who'd

Opposite: Whistlerites have never been shy to let it all hang out. Below: Blackcomb's early success was due in large part to the independent, strong-willed people that Smythe attracted to his team, like Garry Davies (at left, shown here with Hugh).

taken over as head of the Whistler ski patrol in 1967, to see that it got done. "We usually have a pretty solid snowpack in the Coast Mountains," he explains. "But even with all the technology today and the attention paid to forecasting and control, major slides can still occur around here. And when they do, they can be just as deadly as anywhere else on the planet."

Avalanche forecasting and management was still very much an esoteric art in the late '60s. While there was research work being done in Utah, Colorado and California at the time, there was very little information of substance available to ski-area operators in Canada. "Much of the avalanche control that we did had to be based on intuition rather than science," explains Smythe. "And much of it was done on a shoestring budget."

All that was before the Whistler slide of 1972.

Here's how Hugh remembers it: "I was going up Whistler's Green Chair with another patroller. It was snowing lightly, but the weather was pretty mild by Whistler standards. About halfway up the lift, we were suddenly slammed by a fierce snow squall. And I mean fierce. It was like nothing I've ever experienced—before or after." So hard was the squall, in fact, that the lift stopped for a few minutes. "I thought to myself, 'Wow. That's some wind gust.' And then I forgot all about it."

But the storm continued.

Unknown to Hugh at the time, a group of four skiers was making its way along one of the high tracks that traversed Whistler's famous Back Bowls. It was a traverse popular with the mountain's advanced skiers, and not considered unsafe or unduly dangerous. In fact, dozens of other guests had used the same track already that day.

Nobody really knows what happened that afternoon, but Smythe surmises that the snow squall must have been violent enough to destabilize the slope above them. The resulting slide buried them all. "I don't know why exactly, but when we were told later that afternoon that some people were missing, I got a cold chill up my spine," says Smythe. "I knew right away that something serious was amiss."

It took them a long time to find the buried skiers. It took them a long time before they even knew where to look. "It was Jim McConkey who finally discovered the slide path," says Smythe. "So much snow had fallen since the day before that you couldn't even tell there was a fracture there unless you skied over it. And that's exactly what Jim did. After that, finding them was pretty straightforward."

Remembers McConkey: "I had a feeling I'd find something over there. We'd pretty much eliminated any other possibility. It was really the only place to look. Still, I wasn't expecting what I found when I climbed up above the traverse to get a closer look at the upper slopes. It was a huge fracture. A killer."

The slide of '72 marked something of a turning point in Hugh Smythe's life. While he'd always been very focused on the work before, now he became deadly serious about it. "I desperately wanted to find a practical way to deal with this whole avalanche issue," he explains. And the only way he knew how to do that, he says, was get on the road and keep learning. "So I traveled down to the United States and completely immersed myself in what was then considered state-of-the-art. And I learned a huge lesson: No matter how well-developed things were elsewhere, we were strictly on our own when it came to designing control methods that were specific to our region."

It was a lesson that he would apply time and again to Whistler problems during the next 30 years. "That's not to say I didn't gain a great deal from what I was learning," he says. "I traveled a lot, read a lot and learned from some of the best. But I also realized quite soon that I was surrounded by some of the best back home—people like Chris Stethem, John Hetherington and, later, Roger McCarthy. All of these people played a huge role in the development of Whistler in those early years. Their contributions were invaluable."

And they certainly didn't hurt Smythe's ambitions, either. From head of the pro patrol in 1967, he was promoted to safety supervisor two years later. He became hill superintendent in 1970, and finally, hill manager in 1973. "Those were pretty exciting years," he admits. "It seemed back then like we were breaking new ground at every turn."

He remembers, for example, hauling the first portable two-way radio up the mountain. "Compared to what we have now," he says, "it was huge and very heavy." But in those days, there was no communication on the mountain, no connection of any kind between the different lift operators. No matter that the equipment was unwieldy, no matter that it weighed a ton, having the hill manager carry a portable radio was a major improvement on the status quo. "I had ripped a CB radio out of a truck, attached it to a car battery and installed it in my office," explains Smythe. "Fran Dixon was my secretary at the time, so she also became my dispatcher. She had the car radio at the patrol base and I

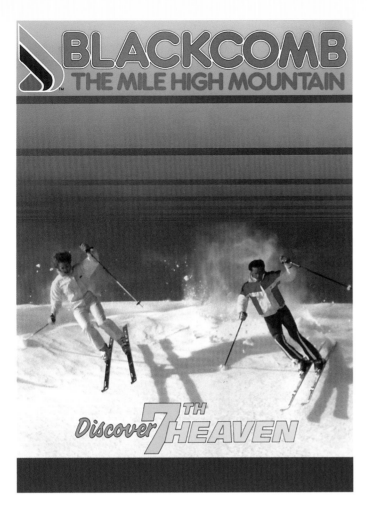

BLACKCOMB
THE MILE HIGH MOUNTAIN

Discover 7TH HEAVEN

Blackcomb's Seventh Heaven promotional page, 1984. Smythe's genius was knowing what people wanted from a ski area—and then going there before any of his competitors did.

had the Johnson portable on the mountain. It wasn't an ideal situation, but it solved a heck of a lot of problems."

By 1974, Smythe was ready for a new challenge. Already he'd felt intuitively that there was a lot more to the business than he was seeing at Whistler. "I wanted to learn more about the total experience. And although I had great respect for Franz Wilhelmsen at the time, I knew his vision did not extend beyond the uphill transportation business. And I needed more."

So when the opportunity arose for Hugh to resurrect a bankrupt ski hill in southwestern Alberta, he fairly jumped at it. "Leaving Whistler was one of the toughest decisions I've ever made," he admits. "But it's also probably one of the most important ones. Going to Fortress Mountain allowed me to get involved in every aspect of the guest experience. And that had a huge impact on me. For at the end of the day, there is a hell of a lot more to the experience than just running a ski lift."

The mandate from the owners—the Federal Business Development Bank (FBDB)—was to turn Fortress Mountain around so that they could get it off their books. But getting Fortress back up and running was no cakewalk. "We didn't get there until early fall," says Smythe. "And we only had a couple of months to rebuild the operation. The place was a shambles. The lifts had been shut down for three years already, and cables and chairs were lying all over the ground, rusting. People had broken into the main lodge and gutted it. It was pretty depressing, in fact."

Despite the ambient mess, Smythe and his two partners, Dave and Lynn Matthews, managed to get the place running smoothly again.

"That's when we brought Aspen into the picture," says Smythe. "I told the folks at the FBDB that Aspen was the biggest player in the ski business, and it was the only one with pockets deep enough to be interested."

And it was—as surprising as that may sound to us today. Seemingly overnight, Aspen Skiing Co. became

a 50 percent owner of Fortress Mountain. And Hugh Smythe got a brand-new boss. "It was kind of a backwards move for me at first," he admits. "I went from working for one uphill transportation company to working for another uphill transportation company." Fortunately, there was too much going on in Colorado at the time for the Aspen bosses to throw anything more than a cursory glance at their new acquisition in Canada. Thus, the young manager was left pretty much to his own devices.

And he took full advantage of it. Smythe managed Fortress Mountain for five years. And he made a great name for himself as a hard-working—and creative—operator. But through all that time, he never stopped thinking of Whistler. "I knew I'd go back eventually. I just wasn't sure how or when that would happen."

He didn't have long to wait. In 1978, the B.C. government put out a call for development proposal bids for Whistler's immediate neighbor, Blackcomb Mountain. The brainchild of former national team coach Al Raine, Blackcomb Mountain was just the project Smythe needed to bring him back home. As big and bold as its 7,160-foot neighbor, Blackcomb was an alpine diamond in the rough. More importantly, it was an ideal place for Smythe to test out all his newborn theories on "the full experience."

"I knew what kind of an impact Blackcomb could have on the ski business," he says. "And I definitely had some strong ideas about how it should be managed." But could he win the bid?

The next few months were wild ones for the 30-year-old. Allied at first with his longtime Whistler pal Paul Matthews (the president of Ecosign Mountain Resort Planners) and a development group from Calgary, Alberta, by the name of Cascade, Smythe had to do some very fancy dancing when his bosses in Aspen announced that they, too, were interested in bidding on the Blackcomb project. What side would he support?

"It was another really tough decision," he admits. "But in the end, I decided to stick with Aspen." Ironically, there were only two bidders for the project: Aspen Skiing Co. (through their Fortress Mountain subsidiary) and the Cascade Group (through the newly formed Blackcomb Skiing Corp). On October 12, 1978, the B.C. government released their decision: Fortress Mountain had won the bid. And Hugh Smythe had a brand-new mountain to build.

Time was running short, however, And the principals knew it. Even before the government had announced the

bid winner, Smythe and his buddy-turned-rival Paul Matthews had decided to go ahead and get some of the preliminary work done on the mountain. "There was no time to waste," says Smythe. "We needed a road cut to the summit before winter hit so we could get up there and do snow studies that year. So Paul and I agreed that whoever won the bid would end up responsible for the cost."

"It was more than a little intimidating," Smythe admits. "I mean, running a ski hill is one thing. But building one from scratch—designing runs, cutting trails, hiring logging companies—involves making really big, and costly, decisions. We had to be on time and on budget to open in December 1980, and privately, I was scared stiff that I couldn't pull it off."

The next two years went by in a blur for Smythe. "It's hard to look back and not laugh," he admits. By all accounts, it was guerilla development at its best. "I had a fuel tank in my front yard at White Gold and a pickup and an old Tucker snowcat parked in my driveway. Our laundry room was the office. Every day we'd ride up the mountain on the road that [legendary Whistler logger] Seppo Makkinen had cut for us. When the snow got deep enough, we simply plowed it with the snowcat and used the Tucker from then on."

Smythe admits he got lost more often on Blackcomb during those first years than he cares to remember. "But at least I learned how to read topographic maps and use a compass."

Bit by bit, the new area started to take shape. By opening day, December 6, 1980, nearly two dozen fall-line runs had been cut, providing roughly 350 acres of skiable terrain, five chairlifts had been built, a base facility was completed and a roomy summit restaurant—the Rendezvous Lodge—was ready for its first visitors. But Hugh was still not content. "We'd started from scratch and built something that worked," he explains. "It was all nicely integrated. And the intermediate cruising was splendid. But that was all we had. We just didn't have enough variety in our run mix. And in my mind, variety still outweighs good design. So I knew that we were going to be the underdog."

The challenge for Smythe then became simple: How could Blackcomb compete with the more established Whistler on terms other than variety of terrain? "So we focused instead on marketing and customer service," he says. "From day one, we'd decided that we were going to be a customer-service organization, and that's where we felt we could make a real difference. As long as we

Opposite: **Smythe at base of Wizard Lift. With a powerful infusion of cash from new owner Intrawest, Smythe put together a Blackcomb redesign that changed the face of skiing in the Whistler Valley forever.** Below: **Blackcomb access road in the late '70s. Challenges were never obstacles for Smythe. They were merely issues to overcome.**

At play in the Blackcomb backcountry.
Smiley Nesbitt on Disease Ridge.

Mike Atkinson drops off
Blackcomb mountain.

THE TOAD HALL POSTER:
MARKING THE END OF AN ERA

I couldn't believe it. There I was, sitting in Kitzbühel's Londoner Pub, at the epicenter of the weeklong Hahnenkamm downhill celebrations, staring at a mutilated Toad Hall poster behind the bar. And there they were—friends and acquaintances—standing proudly in front of the old Soo Valley mill known as Toad Hall in all their naked glory. I took another long swig of beer. "So," I addressed the bartender, pointing at the poster, "Toulouse has been here already, eh?"

He laughed. "Yeah. Yeah. Toulouse is an old friend of the Londoner's. We tell everyone who asks that it's a poster of the Canadian national downhill team." And then he laughed again.

It wasn't ever meant to be an icon. Barely made it into poster form, in fact. In the spring of 1973, when Chris Speedie and Terry "Toulouse" Spense decided to pose 14 naked young people in front of the old mill cabin that they'd soon have to abandon, they just thought it would be a fun thing to do. Besides, why not commemorate Whistler's golden era with yet another naked-hippie picture?

"Things were changing fast at Whistler in those years," says Toulouse. "We'd had a good run, but we could all sense that we were nearing the end of it. I knew that if we didn't capture some of these scenes for posterity, all of it would eventually be forgotten."

One of the valley's more enduring characters, Toulouse has always managed to insert himself into the thick of the action: from working as a special start coach for the Crazy Canucks downhill team in the 1980s to being Prince Charles' ski guide during the British royal's visit to Whistler in 1998. Today, Toulouse runs a bed-and-breakfast lodge at Whistler with his wife, Ann, when he's not too busy shepherding VIP clients around the mountain. And he loves nothing better than to reminisce about the old days.

Whether by coincidence or astral convergence, Whistler Mountain came into its own pretty much during the heyday of the counterculture movement on the West Coast. Influenced to a great extent by San Francisco and the California scene, Vancouver was already considered a northern outpost for adventurous hippies looking for a place to groove. Whistler was simply its mountain extension.

By the early 1970s, the word was out. If you liked powder snow, good smoke and a fun crowd of people, Whistler was the place to be. And though a scathing article about 24-hour drug orgies, free love and pot-addled skiers had appeared in an influential Toronto news magazine and scandalized thousands, it also served to motivate hundreds of young skiers to head west and try their luck in Whistler.

After all, how could you beat quotes like: "Vancouver mothers don't like their daughters to come skiing at Whistler. Because if they meet us bums...they might disappear and not be heard from till spring."

Scandalous, for sure. But alluring, too, if you were young and wild and looking for a cool mountain town to move to. But it wasn't doing much for the more conservative-minded citizens of the young community. Having a good time was all fine and good, they argued. But attracting a reputation as a haven for free sex and drugs just wouldn't work.

One of the first casualties in the new war for respectability was the cluster of buildings that constituted the Soo Valley Logging Company holdings at the north end of Green Lake. Used over the years by a ragtag group of Whistler locals as home, headquarters and party-central, it was slated for destruction in the summer of 1973. Thus the hastily assembled crowd of free spirits—and the history-making photo.

"It was Speedie's idea to make a poster of it," says Toulouse. "He was convinced we could sell a bunch of them—and make a profit, too."

Soon the posters began migrating outside the Whistler Valley. A favorite in ski-bum bathrooms from Jackson Hole to Val d'Isère, they also appeared in the most unlikely of spots. And that, too, was due to Toulouse's influence. During his stint with the Canadian downhill team, Toulouse made sure he got them posted in all the right places—from Kitzbühel's Londoner Pub to St. Anton's Krazy Kangaroo. I even found one once in the staff lodging at the Hotel Portillo in Chile.

"It was the least I could do," says Toulouse, with the most disarming of grins. "It was a time in Whistler's story that should never be forgotten."

The Toad Hall poster hangs in some of the ski world's most prestigious bars.

offered great food, friendly service and a memorable experience, I felt confident that we could compete with anybody in the business."

He smiles. "In fact, our mission statement—creating memories for our guests and our staff—evolved from this. It's on the back of my business cards, and it is as meaningful to me today as it was 22 years ago."

It didn't take long for people to take notice. "It was apparent from the very start that there was something different going on at Blackcomb," says longtime Vancouver skier Nancy Edmonds. "It wasn't so much the big things. It was the details—like tissue dispensers at the bottom of the lifts, and food quality, even the way the Blackcomb staff related to their guests."

And Hugh's guiding hand could be discerned just about everywhere, sometimes quite literally. "I remember the first weekend Blackcomb opened for business," says Nancy Greene-Raine, who was director of skiing at the time. "At the end of the day, there was a huge traffic jam down in the valley. So the staff was directed to keep guests entertained in the base lodge as long as possible. There was free cocoa and snacks and lots of laughter. We must have kept people up there well past six o'clock." Eventually she, too, made it to her car and into the stream of traffic.

"By the time I reached the bottleneck," remembers Greene-Raine, "I noticed that someone with a Blackcomb staff jacket was directing traffic." It was Smythe, doing what he could to alleviate the stress of his guests. "That's always been his management style," says Greene-Raine. "Get in there and get the job done—no matter who you are."

The first few years of operation were tough, however. A crippling snow drought followed by an even more crippling recession nearly sank the upstart resort in its inaugural year. While Smythe's projections had called for 225,000 skier visits that first winter, the mountain recorded barely 52,000.

Franz Wilhelmsen, who had opposed the Blackcomb development (as well as Whistler Mountain's north-side expansion), seemed to be correct in his initial assessment. "There will never be enough business here to support two separate ski areas," he had predicted in 1978. "And we will never become a major destination resort—not with the kind of weather we get here."

As far as he was concerned, it was far better to concentrate on the regional market.

"After all," he said, "you can't expect people to leave Colorado to come skiing here instead."

Above: Chateau Whistler under construction. The decision by CP Hotels to build one of its prestigious Chateaux at the base of Blackcomb was one of the cornerstones of Whistler's recovery. Opposite: One of the first resorts to welcome snowboarders to its slopes, Blackcomb continues to be a hotbed of riding talent.

Meanwhile, Whistler Village, which had started with such promise, was becoming something of an investment graveyard. Projects were halted in mid construction. Cement and rebar and abandoned foundations littered the new village. "It looked like a war zone for a couple of years," says Smythe. "This incredible dream that we'd fostered over the last few years was quickly turning into a nightmare."

Smythe's problems were just beginning. With Blackcomb's rough start, Aspen began to have doubts about its Canadian investments. And with the recession continuing to eat up big chunks of the B.C. economy, it looked increasingly imprudent to pour even more money into the ailing resort. As early as 1983, Aspen's shareholders began to make noises about unloading their unwieldy white elephant. But buyers were hard to find.

Never one to dwell on the negatives, Smythe focused his energies rather on making his ski area even more attractive to customers. "One of the biggest hits against us in the early years," he explains, "was that our skiing terrain still lacked variety. People kept telling me: 'Your runs are boring.' And they were right."

Although Smythe and his lieutenants continued to open up new terrain below timberline, it wasn't until the winter of 1985 that they came up with a radical plan that would change skiing forever in the Whistler Valley. And it would have never happened if Smythe hadn't listened to his subordinates, Rich Morten, Blackcomb's vice president of operations, and Peter Xhignesse, its avalanche forecaster. "I was skeptical at first," admits Smythe. "Their suggestion was to build a lift that climbed high into the alpine, but on the mountain's south-facing slope. And on its windward side, too. Initially, it didn't make a lot of sense to me."

But Smythe was also a risk-taker. And he quickly realized what was at stake. "If we could pull this off, we would become the ski resort with the biggest vertical drop in North America—over 5,000 feet." Besides, he concluded, the lift would access the kind of high-alpine terrain that would ensure no one could ever accuse Blackcomb of being boring again.

He wasn't getting much support from Aspen, however. Nonetheless, Hugh decided to go ahead with the plan. There was a fairly new (but little-used) T-bar at Fortress Mountain, he remembered, that could be dismantled quickly and brought west to Blackcomb. It would be relatively cheap to install and would serve as a test piece for the viability of the new terrain.

"We didn't want any of our Fortress customers to clue in that we were moving lifts off the mountain," he says, "so we got the job done in a day and a half. It just sort of disappeared." And reappeared in pieces a few weeks later on the south slope of Blackcomb Peak. And what a job that was. The fall of 1985 was one of the coldest and stormiest on record. "What should have taken us a month to complete, took us nearly three, instead. It was brutal work."

But Smythe's travails were far from over. Denied funding for the project by his bosses in Aspen, he decided to mount an aggressive marketing campaign to boost season-pass sales and thereby pay for the lifts. Thus was born the "Mile-High Mountain" campaign. For only $480 dollars, screamed the ads, you got access all winter long to the biggest mountain on the continent.

And it worked. Vancouver people bought into the campaign in a big way. Blackcomb Mountain suddenly had a very visible signature. And Whistler as a resort suddenly became more than just a dream. The place was beginning to take off.

"That was a huge turning point for us," says Smythe. But the biggest turning point was yet to come.

By January 1986, it was clear to everyone involved that Aspen was no longer interested in being involved with Blackcomb Mountain. A sale would have to be engineered soon. But investors had been burned at Whistler before—buyers were still hard to find.

One evening, Smythe found himself sitting across the table from Intrawest's Joe Houssian at a Young Presidents Organization meeting. Houssian, an innovative, Vancouver-based real-estate developer, had been extremely successful and was looking to diversify his business. Smythe had just the thing for him. "Joe told me he had learned to ski on the beginner slope at Blackcomb," recounts Smythe. "So talk soon turned to the sale of the ski area—and the generous development rights attached to that sale."

Smythe's legacy is huge. His influence is enormous. Yet Smythe can still be found in the tiny corner office across from the base of the Blackcomb lifts.

Generous indeed. Included in the sale package was a total of 254 acres of zoned property in the Benchlands area directly adjacent to the mountain, as well as the right to build 7,500 commercial beds on that land. What was there not to like about the deal?

To his credit, Houssian could see much further down the road than the folks at the Aspen Skiing Co. On August 1, 1986, Intrawest bought Aspen's 50 percent share of Blackcomb, as well as an option to buy the Federal Business Development Bank's 50 percent stake over the next five years.

The corner had finally been turned. A new operations/development philosophy was set in motion that day that would—over the next 10 years—completely revolutionize the way mountain resorts were built, operated and marketed in North America. For better or worse, Blackcomb Mountain—and Whistler Resort— would never be the same again.

And Smythe and Houssian were not about to relinquish their momentum. Less than a year later, the newly reaffirmed president of Blackcomb Mountain announced a $26 million facelift to the six-year-old resort that included an integrated network of high-speed detachable quad chairlifts, a new base lodge, more extensive snow making and a long list of smaller improvements.

It was probably the most effective real-estate promotional tool in resort development history. As soon as the work on the mountain started, Intrawest began developing its Benchlands properties. The first 130 recreational units were snapped up immediately—$200,000 condos went like hotcakes. By the spring of 1988, with Canadian Pacific Railway's historic decision to build one of its "Chateaux" a mere stone's throw away from the Blackcomb lifts, the resort was booming again.

For more than 20 years, Hugh Smythe had been travelling around Europe and North America—"going to school," he called it—trying to learn how the best resorts in the world were managed. "I learned so much from going on these trips," he says. "Benchmarking is extremely important to us as a company. It always has been."

By the early '90s, many of the resort operators who hosted Smythe in the '70s and '80s were beating a path to his door to learn from him and his staff. And while he was far from smug about the change in roles, it certainly gave him a lot of pleasure. "It truly is fun to see people coming to "school" here now— especially when many of them come from places where I first started my studies."

In recent years, the trickle of "students" has become a flood. And they come to Whistler from every corner of the globe—the United States, Japan, Korea, Austria, Switzerland and France—to learn how Smythe and Intrawest manage to stay so far ahead of the competition.

Still, the last thing he wants to do is become complacent. "The reason that Whistler-Blackcomb is so far ahead of the pack today," he says, "is that we're still focused on the total experience—and that includes everything from employee housing to our food and beverage service. And we can't ever lose that focus."

He laughs. "Even when you're the leader in your field, you've got to know exactly what your competitors are doing. And you have to identify clearly what they're doing that is better than what you're doing at home. Otherwise, you just stay in the same place. No matter where I am or what I'm working on, one question remains paramount in my mind: How can I use my 'studies' to improve the total experience back home? Because it's quite simple. When you stop learning, you grow old and inflexible. And everything becomes stagnant."

And he knows just how high the stakes have become. "Today, the resort is so well-balanced (from a planning standpoint) that the next move is a very sensitive one. Anything we decide to do from this point on has enormous consequences."

He sighs. And for just a moment his warrior's mask slips a little.

"We want to be absolutely sure," he concludes, "that we continue to make all the right decisions as we grow and expand."

A FORMIDABLE TEAM

CHAPTER 5
AL RAINE & NANCY GREENE

She was Canada's golden girl. Her ski racing accomplishments—an Olympic gold medalist in 1968 and overall World Cup champion in '68 and '69—made her a household name at home and abroad. Tough and fiercely competitive—they called her Tiger—she was a small-town girl with a big-time agenda. And she was just what the country needed. Call it good timing. Or good luck. Or simply hard work and strong genes. After her retirement from racing, Nancy Greene managed to leverage her skiing victories into one of the most successful product-endorsement careers in Canada. And she never forgot her roots. Skiing wasn't just a sport for Tiger. It was a way of life.

Al Raine's resume was no less impressive. The mastermind behind the Canadian Alpine Ski Team's rise to prominence in the mid '70s, he was widely respected across the ski racing world for his breadth of knowledge and political smarts. But ski-racing was only one of his interests. Passionate about mountain-resort design—and outspoken about the need to bring more "soul" to the North American ski-resort model—Al had one abiding dream: to build his own ski resort in B.C.

As husband and wife, Al and Nancy would become one of the most influential couples on the Canadian ski scene. Both B.C.-born and raised, they succeeded in bringing a new global perspective to what had been, traditionally, a fairly parochial business. As for their impact on Whistler, many believe the resort would not be what it is today were it not for Al Raine's drive and vision.

"There were many important players involved in the development of Whistler," says Intrawest's Hugh Smythe. "But I think Al, more than anyone else, had a clear picture of what this place would look like when it was all built out. He was definitely a guiding light during a very complex time."

But let's start at the beginning.

In the intimate little world of Canadian ski racing, Al and Nancy's marriage in 1969 was the alpine equivalent of a royal wedding. A former racer who had spent three years pursuing his skiing passions in Europe, Al had just been hired as program director for the Canadian Alpine Ski Team. Nancy had retired from ski racing the year before and was now hard at work learning the ins and outs of the business world. "It was pretty simple," she says. "I met Al, fell in love with him, and we were married soon after." She laughs. "He is a unique person. As surprising as this may sound, Al has never been driven by monetary gain. And in this business, that's a definite asset, because you're not always rewarded in money."

Although the national team offices were in Montreal, the Raines decided they wanted to establish a base of operations on the West Coast as well. And Whistler in 1969 looked like an ideal place for the newlyweds to put some roots down. "Al had been managing a summer training camp on Kokanee Glacier in the interior of B.C.," remembers Nancy. When the camp was moved to

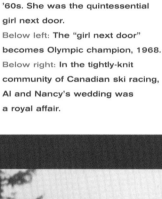

Opposite: **Nancy with American champion Jimmie Heuga in the '60s. She was the quintessential girl next door.**
Below left: **The "girl next door" becomes Olympic champion, 1968.**
Below right: **In the tightly-knit community of Canadian ski racing, Al and Nancy's wedding was a royal affair.**

Whistler Mountain, and Olympic gold medalist Toni Sailer was hired to work there, Nancy decided she'd like to coach on the glacier, too. "Which meant that both Al and I would now be working at Whistler for most of the off-season," she explains. "So we built a [cabin] in White Gold Estates and moved in for the summer."

Nancy was already pregnant by then. In January 1970, she gave birth to twin boys, Charlie and Willie. Soon after, the Raines decided to move their brood west. They bought a house next door to Al's parents in Burnaby, a suburb of Vancouver, and Al commuted back and forth between Vancouver and Montreal. "It was a great extended-family setting," says Nancy. "And for the kids, it was really wonderful. But Al was still traveling a lot in those years, so our family time was mostly spent at our Whistler cabin during the off-season."

By 1973, Al was beginning to tire of the road-warrior lifestyle. Besides, after five years at the helm, he felt his job was done in Montreal. The national team program (not yet 10 years old) was now well established, a group of young Canadian skiers was just beginning to make its mark on the international scene, and the Nancy Greene Ski League—a new coast-to-coast racing program for preteens—was doing wonders for the sport.

More importantly, though, Al had this other dream he wanted to pursue.

"By now, I'd traveled extensively in Europe—particularly in Austria and Switzerland—and I was convinced that the mountains and snow of B.C. were vastly superior. But there was still no heart and soul to our mountain developments. We had no community, no sense of culture. In essence, we didn't know what a mountain village was all about. And I kept asking myself: 'Why not?'"

So he decided to see what he could do to change it.

Nancy, meanwhile, had been tending to her family in Burnaby. Now her focus, too, moved to the mountains. "We began spending a lot more time at Whistler," she says. "But I was still mostly busy with the kids. I was the designated homemaker." Somehow, it's hard to imagine Nancy sitting at home making soup. Which is why she was so excited to be spending more time at Whistler. "It didn't take me long to get involved in the goings-on of the community."

She also became increasingly involved in her husband's new projects. "Al's always called me his secret weapon," she confides. And then she laughs. "We're a pretty good team together. Between us, we can get a lot done."

Above: Nancy with summer race camp directors (left to right) Allan White, Roy Ferris, and Toni Sailer. Although she'd raced there before, Nancy got her first real taste of Whistler Mountain as one of the "celebrity" coaches at the Toni Sailer Summer Camp.
Opposite: Ski touring high above the Callaghan Valley. Al and Nancy's early dream was to establish a ski area at Powder Mountain, only a few miles down valley from Whistler.

Indeed. Nancy has never been afraid to act on her own gut feelings. And B.C. skiing has always been something that she's believed in with heart and soul. In 1967, for example, she jeopardized her World Cup lead by staying home from two European meets to race at Whistler (then barely into its second year of operations). "It's who I am," she says simply. "I've always known just how special this province is. And I've always been proud to promote it."

While her B.C.-first attitude has often been derided by critics as a ploy to promote her husband's development plans, Nancy insists her motives have never been financially motivated. In a 1975 interview, she was quite blunt about it. "If it was just about money," she said, "I wouldn't be here. I'd be in the States."

The couple's first mountain-development project came within a hair of being approved. Located just south of Whistler in the stunningly scenic Callaghan Valley, Powder Mountain had all the prerequisites that Al thought were necessary for success: good snow, right exposure, ideal altitude and just enough level land in the valley to construct a cozy base village. Sadly, the project foundered on the government's unwillingness to invest in a $3 million access road.

That's when Al and Nancy started looking closer to home. And it didn't take long for them to see what nearby Blackcomb Mountain had to offer. "Anybody with a brain could appreciate the development potential there," says Nancy. "With its regular fall line and long runouts, it was obvious it would make an ideal ski area. Besides, this time around, we didn't need the government's help to build us a road. We just needed right-of-ways and such."

So Al decided to contact B.C.'s minister of lands again and try to get the development process started for Blackcomb. "They were just beginning to log the lower slopes of the mountain at the time," remembers Al. "And I thought that was crazy. So I wrote a pretty strongly worded letter to Bob Williams [B.C.'s then minister of lands], outlining my thoughts on Blackcomb's potential."

Two weeks later, Williams contacted Al to say he wanted to meet with him to discuss where Al thought the skiing might work on Blackcomb. Almost overnight, Al recalls with a laugh, logging stopped on the mountain. "Suddenly, the trucks started coming down off Blackcomb," he says, "And that, I can tell you, was a major turning point in the Whistler story."

Even today, nearly three decades later, Al still gets excited when talk turns to the early Whistler years.

He's not a big man—in fact, he's quite slight. And he's not loud or insistent. On the contrary. He's almost courtly. Understated even. But the passion of his ideas is evident in his every word. This is a subject he could talk about all day. And it's a subject that he knows more about than most.

"My vision for Whistler came from what I'd learned in the Alps," he explains. "We had the snow and the mountains. But what we badly needed was a people place—a pedestrian village—within easy walking distance to the lifts." He laughs. "I thought if we could develop that model at Whistler, we would become world leaders in mountain tourism."

At the time, the Whistler valley was nowhere near that model. A scraggly conglomeration of Gothic-arched cabins spreading like a bad fungus on either side of Highway 99, Alta Lake in the early '70s was a disaster waiting to happen. Nobody seemed to have an overriding plan for the valley. And nobody seemed to care much. Speculation was rampant. Real-estate developers were circling for the kill. Yet single family lots could still be had for under $10,000.

A 1975 article in a Vancouver newspaper paints a fairly bleak picture of the valley: "Visitors who finally make it [to Whistler] expecting chalets nestled behind a cafe-lined main street are bound to be disappointed. The only chalets are privately owned in four or five subdivisions strung out along six miles of highway, a main street where logging trucks rarely slow below 60 mph as they speed between Pemberton and Squamish. Nightlife? Well, there are Saturday dances, B-grade movies and a pub, often short of beer, where the shouts of a bartender are the only thing louder than the jukebox."

Meanwhile, there still was no bank, no grocery store and no post office. And no sewage system, either. Property owners—both private and commercial—were responsible for their own waste disposal. And "responsibility" was not a particularly respected concept at Whistler during those years.

"You know how this whole thing started, don't you?" asks Nancy. At 57, Nancy Greene-Raine is still just as forceful as she was back in her racing days. She's always had an edge to her personality. And she doesn't suffer fools. But she has a soft spot for Whistler that she just can't camouflage. "It's simple," she continues. "The lakes—the jewels of this valley—were getting polluted from all the development. We could see it with our own eyes. And we needed to do something quick. We needed a plan. A vision

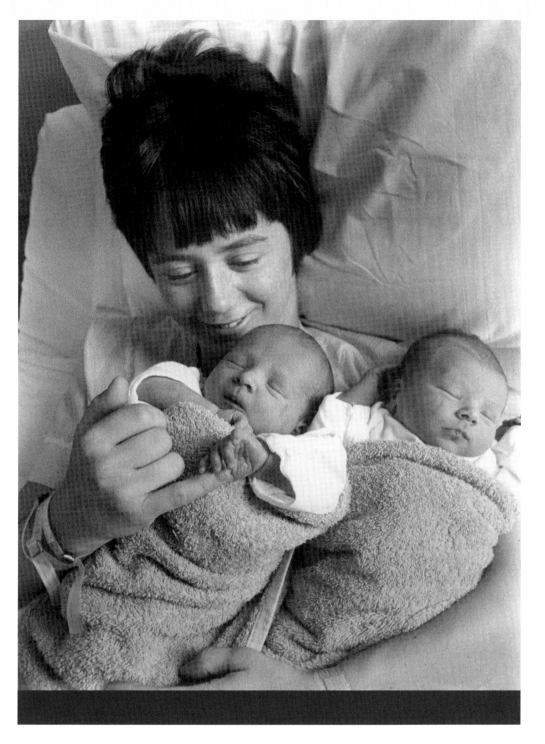

Nancy with sons Charlie and Willie (1970). She won two World Cups in a row and then promptly gave birth to twin sons. Nancy was never one for taking the easy route.

about the need for a centrally located village to act as a cultural glue for the young community. "I was the guy with the pie-in-the-sky ideas," says Al. "But Garry could work with these ideas on a practical level. His expertise as a lawyer was really valuable." From that initial meeting grew a lifelong friendship.

"We had a pretty dynamic little community," remembers Nancy. "We were all still pretty young at the time—in our early 30s—and we thought we were invincible. There were some real battles. But generally, we all got along surprisingly well. Somehow, for the first few years at least, it was a real team process."

Al showed up at his meeting with Lands Minister Bob Williams with a broad proposal: "For me, it was a very straightforward proposition. Before us was the future of the Whistler Valley. And in my mind, it could only go one way: two mountains linked by a pedestrian village whose shops are owned by small-scale entrepreneurs with a passion for mountain life."

Two weeks later—in May 1975—Williams contacted the Raines with a proposal of his own. But it wasn't quite what Al was expecting. Rather than Al becoming a developer, the minister wanted Raine to become B.C.'s first coordinator of ski development. And it meant setting some serious precedents. Remembers Nancy: "Bob Williams told Al: 'We don't have any policies for developing new ski areas in this province. Given your expertise in this field, we've decided we want you to devise those policies for us.' It was quite an honor. But it was also a monstrous undertaking."

Aside from developing and writing B.C.'s first-ever commercial alpine ski policy—a document that would introduce the revolutionary 'land-for-lifts' concept for ski area developers—Raine would also be responsible for drafting the proposal calling for the development of Blackcomb Mountain. Finally, he would act as an advisor to the Municipal Affairs Department while it prepared special legislation for the incorporation of Whistler.

After talking it over with Nancy, Al decided to put his own entrepreneurial aspirations aside and accept the newly created position. "I took a deep breath," says Al, "and stepped right into the storm."

Not long after he was hired, the B.C. legislature passed the long-sought Resort Municipality of Whistler Act. Whistler would be managed by a modified form of municipal government in which property owners and residents were responsible for electing a mayor and three aldermen. The province would be represented on the council by one

for the future. We needed to figure out how to manage this place before we completely destroyed it."

Her husband had seen an early plan for Whistler prepared by B.C.'s Department of Municipal Affairs. And it scared him. "The government's plan was all about big hotels and cold beds, which is exactly what we didn't want. We needed to have smaller properties where people with passion could get involved."

It was around this time—"at a Whistler zoning meeting, I believe," says Al—that the Raines met Garry Watson. A Vancouver lawyer, and a passionate Whistlerite in his own right, Watson was just as concerned as they were over Whistler's lack of a unifying vision. Furthermore, he shared many of Al's opinions

government-appointed alderman, who would retain veto power, oversee the community's financial dealings and generally take care of the province's interest.

Not surprisingly, Al Raine served as the first government-appointed alderman.

"The creation of the resort municipality of Whistler was a revolutionary act," insists Nancy. "For suddenly the community had a real voice. And it had political clout as well. Now we could finally begin to get things moving in the right direction."

"My first job," recalls Al, "was to get the community on board with our plans for the future. We held dozens of meetings. Brought in all sorts of experts to put our vision in context." He pauses. "But we also had some immediate physical issues to deal with, too—like creating a comprehensive sewage system for the valley."

As complex as it was, building the new sewer system was by far the easier task. For getting the disparate Whistler groups to agree on one vision for the future was a decidedly tough nut to crack. "Essentially," says Raine, "there were two diametrically opposed views. The first was a multi-modal design plan that advocated the creation of many small villages throughout the valley. The second was the single-centered vision of one

principal village linking the two mountains."

Already in 1974, the government had come out in favor of the latter. And while many Whistlerites bought into the village-between-two-mountains proposal, it was far from a unanimous decision. "I'll never forget the community meeting when the village site was first discussed," says Nancy. "I remember Franz Wilhelmsen got up and said: 'Are you all crazy? This will never work. This place is too isolated, too wet and too stormy, for it to ever fly as an international destination resort.'"

More insidious, however, was a very vocal group of land developers, who had seen their plans for quick profits foiled when the government had imposed a land freeze at Whistler in 1974, advocating a very different vision than the "official" one. Under the banner of the Whistler Development Association (WDA), they aggressively lobbied against the government's one-center model. As far as they were concerned, the only viable plan was one that spread the wealth throughout the valley by creating a number of smaller, more diversified centers.

Things got really hot when, after elections in the fall of 1975, there was suddenly a new B.C. government in power. For a while, it looked as if the developers' group, the WDA, might have the upper hand. "It really came down to

Above: Al Raine, far left, at a '70s Whistler meeting, with John Hetherington (next to Raine) and Garry Watson (arm on table). Al knew intuitively that creating a village at the base of two mountains like Whistler and Blackcomb would transform this B.C. backwater into a world-class destination. It just took time to convince everyone else of that. Opposite: Al checks his mountain-top weather station. A passionate researcher, Al Raine knows more about the Coast Mountains than just about any other living person.

It was clear that Nancy Greene-Raine and my daughter Maya had hit it off. "Don't worry," said the doyenne of Canadian ski racing, "Maya is going to ski down in my group. She'll be fine."

"Yeah, dad. Don't worry, I'll be fine," echoed my then seven-year-old daughter, as she wrestled her feet into her bindings. "And you know what, dad? Nancy said that I could ski right behind her all the way down to the bottom. It's going to be so cool."

Like two young schoolmates, they disappeared into the gloom, still yakking away like they'd known each other forever.

I was summarily dismissed. Just like that. And I felt a little twitch in the pit of my stomach. It wasn't exactly concern. I knew Maya was in good hands. I also knew she could handle the torchlight descent. Still, didn't she want to do it in the company of her dad?

But it was my own fault. When I was a kid, Nancy Greene was my hero. Still is, in a lot of ways. So when I decided to take my young family to visit the Raines at Sun Peaks back in 1996, I didn't hesitate to tell Maya and her sister, Jenna, the story of the B.C. kid who took on the ski racing world and won.

Born and raised in Rossland, one of Canada's few genuine mountain towns, Nancy started skiing on nearby Red Mountain when she was three. "We skied all over the place," she remembers, "especially through the funny little trails, the dips and jumps and bumps through the woods. Just skiing down the hill was a little boring because I liked to go fast and wasn't scared of the slope."

Ski racing was a family passion with the Greenes. A community thing, even. After all, skiing was part of their cultural fabric. It was what Rosslanders did. Racing was just another way of celebrating that culture.

Following in her older sister's footsteps, Nancy quickly made a name for herself on the local ski racing circuit. By 1960 and the Olympic Games in Squaw Valley, California, the 16-year-old was the youngest member of a strong Canadian women's team that included eventual gold medalist Ann Heggtveit.

"What an experience that was," Nancy says. "I was so overwhelmed by all the pomp and circumstance, it was hard to concentrate on the racing."

Still she finished 22nd in the downhill, second best among Canadians. She improved to seventh by 1964 and the Innsbruck Olympics. But she was still not satisfied with her performance. "I knew in my heart I could be the best. I just knew I'd have to work darn hard for it."

Which she did. By the 1968 season, she was ranked number one in the world. But a harrowing crash only a few weeks before the Grenoble Games—at a World Cup race in her hometown— almost dashed her hopes for Olympic glory. But Greene would not be denied. After a slow start in the downhill (her best event), she worked her way up to second place in the slalom and then decimated the competition in the giant slalom, winning the event—and the gold medal—by a whopping 2.64 seconds. She retired that spring after being crowned World Cup champion for the second year in a row.

Clearly, my daughter Maya had taken the story to heart. She had hardly left Nancy's side all evening. As for Nancy, I suspect she might have seen a little of herself in the sun-kissed mountain girl with the freshly braided hair. I don't think she minded the attention at all.

And, of course, the evening's finale went off just fine. The torchlight descent from the top of Sun Peaks was a hit with both of them. They even made a date to go skiing together the next day.

"You know, dad," Maya said to me later. "Nancy wasn't at all what I expected. I thought she'd be this really serious older person. But she didn't seem old to me. We had a lot of fun talking and skiing together. I think she's what you'd call 'young at heart'. Do you think so, dad?"

No question.

With happy campers on
Whistler Mountain. Nancy
was always at her best
around kids.

the wire," says Al. "But after doing a little research, the new government decided that, after all, our plan was the most reasonable one, and they encouraged us to keep going."

And on they went. But they never would have succeeded, says Al, without the special mix of characters serving on Whistler's council during those early years. "For example: Garry Watson was the guy who came up with very practical solutions to many of the 'big-picture' ideas we'd hammered out," he says. "Without Garry, a lot of things would have never happened."

Another key player was Mayor Pat Carlton. "He didn't know a ski resort from a parking lot," says Raine. "But it didn't matter. For he was a very smart guy. And he could talk the paint off a wall. We might come up with all these great concepts. But it was Mayor Carlton who took our ideas and went out and sold the community on the stuff."

Finally, there was John Hetherington, "a hippie who came to Whistler as a ski bum, became a pro patroller and then was voted in as alderman," says Raine. "His role on the council was making sure that what was happening was environmentally sound. He was our conscience. And he could be stubborn as all get out." Al pauses. Smiles. "As unlikely as it may seem now, there was a really good balance between the four of us."

But there were still a number of obstacles for the council to overcome before Whistler would ever see its new village—foremost of which was the way it was going to be laid out. Having set up a special entity, the Whistler Village Land Company, to administer the development of the town-center land, the municipality then began to address the nuts-and-bolts issues of designing a mountain village from scratch.

"The first architectural plans were a dog's breakfast," admits Raine. "It was horrible—like a huge shopping mall."

On a research trip to the United States, the members of the Whistler council had met Vail's town manager, Terry Minger, and had been quite excited about his ideas on mountain communities.

"So we invited him up to Whistler to speak," remembers Raine. "During his visit, I confided to him my concerns that the architects and engineers who were working on the project really didn't understand what mountain resorts were all about. That's when he told me about Eldon Beck. Said he was the best in the business, and I shouldn't hesitate to contact him."

A well-respected landscape architect based in San Francisco, Beck was intrigued with the Whistler project

and soon agreed to join the design team. In the meantime, Raine and Watson had managed to finagle several million dollars out of the federal government to build—among other things—an underground parking network below the new village. It was the last piece in the puzzle.

"I believed strongly at the time that you couldn't deliver on a pedestrian-only village without underground parking," says Raine. "But it was the kind of thing that private developers were not interested in building."

Beck's early sketches looked promising. Introducing such fresh new concepts as view corridors and secondary seating—as well as special covenants that controlled each building parcel on the village site—Beck's model for the new Whistler was just what Raine had hoped for.

The Village under construction, 1979. Luckily recession didn't hit until the contruction was well underway.

"Our vision was to have a town center with a grocery store and a hardware store and a liquor store and a post office," says Raine. "A place, in other words, where the locals, as well as the tourists, shopped. And Eldon didn't disappoint us on that score. His design was exactly what we needed."

And the good news just kept coming. On October 3, 1978, the B.C. government announced that Fortress Mountain Resorts Ltd. had won the right to develop Blackcomb Mountain. Franz Wilhelmsen and Garibaldi Lifts Ltd. were also on board with the plan—although reluctantly—and had agreed to cut runs and build a lift system on Whistler Mountain's north side in order to link up with the new village.

Raine's vision was finally coming to fruition. Little more than three and a half years after he'd agreed to Bob Williams' terms, B.C.'s first coordinator of ski development could point to Whistler with justifiable pride. And he'd managed it just in time. "Had construction on the Whistler Village project been delayed by just a year," he says, "it would have tumbled right into the 1981 recession." He stops talking for a moment. Sighs. "If that had happened, I'm not sure that Whistler Village would have ever been completed."

By the fall of 1980, everything was in place. Two brand-new mountain complexes were about to open their doors to the public. The village already boasted a grocery store, a pharmacy, a deli and a neighborhood pub. And new lots in the Phase Two development were selling well. There was a buzz in the valley that year among residents that had never been there before.

"A lot of people outside Whistler didn't think it could ever happen—that we were going to fail dismally," remembers Nancy. "So it was really exciting to watch it all go up around us."

The Raines had become full-time Whistler residents some years before, and now Nancy was fully immersed in community life. Following in the footsteps of Myrtle Philip, she'd become a school trustee for the district—a region that stretched from Squamish in the south to Pemberton in the north. "There were some epic struggles in those years between 'the uppity young people at Whistler' and the 'working folk down-valley.' We had some really big issues to resolve. Like where to locate the new school, for example. But we made it through. And in the end, that's what really matters."

What matters even more, adds Nancy, was the model the Whistler community devised to reach its goals. "The miracle of Whistler, " she says, "was that it managed to meld public and private good together. And that hadn't happened too often in B.C. before."

Unfortunately, the fledgling community was about to be tested severely. First came a brutal snow drought that almost sank Blackcomb.

"It was really depressing," says Nancy, who was hired as the resort's first director of skiing. "Blackcomb was a great mountain. It had wonderful intermediate/advanced terrain where you could make these great carved turns down the fall line. And Hugh [Smythe] was a wonderful leader—a real innovator. But that first winter was a disaster. I still remember sitting in the valley in January, watching the rain wash away what little snow we'd managed to hoard."

Then a recession hit. Considered one of the most severe in the checkered economic history of B.C., it smashed into Whistler with the force of a sledgehammer. By 1982, the real-estate collapse in the valley had reached epidemic proportions. New buildings in the village lay partially finished or empty. New businesses were going bankrupt at an alarming rate. People were walking away from once-lucrative investments. The value of construction in 1982, for example, was $3.85 million. For the same period the year before, the figure had been six times as high.

And the Vancouver media ate it up. Whistler's woes were all self-administered, said the pundits. Those uppity funhogs up in Fantasyland should have known their place. A 1982 editorial put it best: "It's too bad that Whistler's bubble has burst, but that's what often happens when people get over-ambitious and try to do too much too soon. If the village hadn't tried to turn itself into a world resort almost overnight, it wouldn't be in the difficulties it's in now."

Talk about getting kicked when you're down.

For the Raines, Whistler's economic downturn was no better—or worse—than for any other resident in the valley. Al, who had recently resigned his post with the government to become a private consultant, decided to step out of the storm for a while and take a two-year sabbatical. "I knew there was going to be some ugly bloodletting," he says, "and I just didn't feel like being around to see it happen."

"We'd always planned to take our kids to Europe," continues Nancy, "and Al tried to convince me that this would be a great time to do that. But I wasn't so sure at first. I thought it was kind of disloyal of us in some way."

It was only when she raised the subject with her twin sons that she was finally convinced it was time to take a break.

"I said to the boys: 'How would you like to go and live in Switzerland?'" remembers Nancy. "And they asked: 'Will you be coming too?'" She stops talking for a moment. Shakes her head. Takes a deep breath and then continues, "That's when I realized we'd been neglecting our kids. It was definitely time for us to regroup."

By the time the family came back to Canada in the fall of 1984, the worst of the recession had passed. "We drove across the country in a VW van," remembers Al, "and I could see that the economic climate was improving. There was still a lot of doom-and-gloom talk at Whistler, but I could sense the dark mood would soon dissipate. So I told Nancy: 'Let's get in and buy a piece of the future.'" He smiles. "And that's how we got into the hotel business at Whistler."

Nancy Greene's Olympic Lodge opened its doors a year later, in December 1985. "It had been really tough to find investment money for our project," admits Al. "It was extremely frustrating, in fact. But we were confident that we could make this thing happen."

And make it happen they did. As usual, their timing was excellent. Whistler had indeed turned the corner. Once again, business was booming in the village center. With the announcement of the sale of Blackcomb to Intrawest in August 1986, the financial woes of the early '80s were finally relegated to the back closet. Although the municipality still had a bit of a financial puzzle to work out before everything was settled between itself and the provincial government, the scene was now set for healthy future growth.

The Raines happily surfed the new wave of prosperity. And did it with style. Reflecting the couple's experience and taste, Nancy Greene's Olympic Lodge had all the charm and intimacy of a small European pension. Nancy's medals and World Cup trophies were displayed proudly in the atrium of the hotel. Pictures, crests and old racing gear graced the walls. And Nancy herself was a constant presence—greeting guests, skiing with VIPs and generally doing what she was best at: being Nancy Greene. As for Al, he was happiest working behind the scenes, running the lodge's day-to-day business.

"Our plan," he says, "was to operate the hotel for the next 10 years and then retire." He laughs. "But after two years, our door was being banged on nearly

Above: **Whistler Village, 2002. While there are many people who claim credit for Whistler's growth and success, the Raines played an enormous role in its early development.** Opposite: **Nancy and Diamond Jim McConkey. Nancy's greatest legacy may simply be her deep and abiding enthusiasm for the sport.**

No one dreamed how big Whistler
would eventually become.

every day by people making us the most outrageous offers to buy the place."

They finally got an offer they couldn't refuse.

"And so we sold it," says Nancy. There's a long silence. "You don't look back," she says. "Still, I was sad to leave. We'd put a lot of energy into building that place. But once again, the time was right for us to let go."

Besides, Whistler had grown bigger than the Raines were comfortable with. "I was very concerned, right from the very first, that this valley could only support so many people," admits Al. "Yet I wrestled with it because I didn't believe in forcing things by decree." Another pause. "To tell you the truth, I don't really know what the answer is. But when I look at how busy and crowded Whistler has become...well, all I can say is that it's still an unresolved issue with me today."

While the Raines were done with Whistler for the time being, they were far from finished with B.C. resorts. When nearby Tod Mountain was bought by Japanese investors (Nippon Cable), renovated to the tune of many millions of dollars and renamed Sun Peaks, Al and Nancy were the first to be approached to develop one of the cornerstone hotels there. "Al had done some master-plan work at Tod in the past," explains Nancy. "And we couldn't really imagine getting anything going at Whistler anymore. So it was kind of natural for us to cross over the Coast Range and get involved—once again—in some grassroots development."

Their new hotel—Nancy Greene's Cahilty Lodge—sits right at the base of Sun Peaks, barely a stone's throw from the main lift. And while the village is much smaller than its Whistler counterpart, Al and Nancy both agree they are far more comfortable with the scale of development here. "Sun Peaks is starting to make a real name for itself—particularly with the European market," says Nancy. "People come here because it isn't Whistler. It's more intimate. More friendly."

Still, muses Al, none of Sun Peak's success could have happened without the groundbreaking work done at Whistler in the mid '70s. "Whistler is still the engine that pulls the B.C. ski train. After all, that's what put B.C. on the international map in the first place. Without Whistler there would be no Fernie Alpine Resort, no Sun Peaks and no Kicking Horse Mountain Resort, either."

He smiles: "And if only for that, I'm really proud to have played a role in Whistler's early development."

Opposite: First tracks on Blackcomb Glacier. Without Al Raine's vision, this would still be a heli-sking run. Now it's but a short walk from the lifts. Below: Al and Nancy at work promoting their next project. They love skiing. And they love the Coast Mountains. British Columbia wouldn't be the same without them.

CHAPTER
VINCENT MASSEY

The sky outside is the color of dirty linen. Skeins of mist wrap themselves around the tall Douglas firs on the

edge of the property. I'm sitting with Vincent Massey in his living room, high up in Whistler's Alpine Meadows

subdivision. "My earliest memories of Whistler are playing in the parking lot, in the mud, in my rubber boots,"

says my lanky host. Before us, the slopes of Whistler and Blackcomb are perfectly framed in the room's vast

picture window. It feels from this vantage point like we're sitting in a tree fort instead of a house. But a very

comfortable, very luxurious tree fort.

"That was the summer of '65, I think," continues Vincent—known as Binty by his friends—as he gets up and

stokes his wood stove. "It was the year the gondola barn was built. I remember because my dad was already working on some projects up here." And then he laughs—a cross between a bray and a chuckle. "I remember the drive, too—a three-hour trek up this wild network of logging roads from Squamish. You even had to drive across a dam to link up two of the roads. Amazing to think of all that's happened since then."

He laughs again and offers me a piece of home-baked bread. "I just made it this afternoon," he assures me. "A new recipe. I think you'll like it."

And I do. We sip tea and munch on his homemade bread while in front of us, deep in the Fitzsimmons Valley, Fissile Peak and Overlord Mountain play hide-and-seek with a bank of low clouds.

Along with the Walshes and the Frazees, the Quinns, the McPhersons, the Sloans and the Ladners, Binty Massey and his siblings were among the first generation of Vancouver-born kids to grow up on the slopes of Whistler. They weren't full-time residents. Not at first anyway. But they still were deeply touched by their early mountain experiences.

"We built our first cabin here in 1967," says Binty. "I was eight, I guess. It was the biggest house in the valley

back then. We shared it between two families. There was the Massey side. And there was the Frazee side. Eight kids in all; four parents. It was wild!"

"My strongest memories of Whistler," he adds, "are of the massive amounts of snow we used to get. I remember having to dig into our house every Friday afternoon after spending the week in the city. It made the adventure of coming up here all the more exciting."

He also remembers the agonizingly long lift rides to the top of the mountain. "It used to take at least 45 minutes to get to the top," he explains. "We'd be so cold by the time we got off the Red Chair that we'd all go straight into the Roundhouse and warm ourselves around the fireplace for the rest of the day. There would be a whole bunch of us kids there—hanging out or playing cards or just fooling around. And it would drive the adults crazy."

While some of his friends were drawn to ski racing in their youth, Binty was far more interested in exploring the mountain's off-piste offerings. "My father used to do a lot of touring," he says. "And I tagged along as often as I could. Ski racing was fun and stuff. But I far preferred freeskiing. I remember attending a ski camp one summer and Nancy Greene telling me I'd never become a successful ski racer

Above: Binty throwing pots in his workshop. Over the years, he has built a reputation as one of Canada's premier potters. Opposite: The original Whistler gondola. Binty's artistic leanings were manifested early with the gondola cars as his first canvases.

because I liked skiing powder too much. And I remember thinking: 'Yeah, so what's your point?'"

Still, he says, the early ski racing program at Whistler was excellent. "Joe Czismania was our coach. He had this European approach to discipline. He could certainly be tough at times. But he was the best." He pauses for a moment. "We certainly had a lot of fun in those years. It was almost like a little private club up here."

Was this around the time, I wonder, when he started carving his name in the gondola cars?

"I can remember first scratching Binty '69, so I probably started that year," he answers. "By 1972, all the cars were done. I'd covered them all."

The first lift ever built at Whistler, the old Creekside gondola, featured enclosed aluminum cabins that carried four skiers apiece. The cabins' walls were also ideal canvases for young graffiti artists looking to express themselves. And Binty became famous—or infamous—throughout the resort for being so diligent in his efforts.

"You gotta remember," he says with a laugh, "there were a lot of other kids who were doing it, too. I just had a name that everyone could remember."

Today, the former graffiti outlaw is a Whistler institution. A world-renowned potter and longtime arts promoter in the valley; a member of Whistler's vaunted Search and Rescue Team; an inspired trail maker and cofounder of the groundbreaking Whistler Off-Road Cycling Association; and a committed glisse-sport fun-hog who can ski, ride and surf with the best—the 44-year-old father of two is also something of a renaissance man. Not in any kind of conventional way, mind you. More in a Mister Fix-It/Walter-Mittyish/survivalist 21st-century kind of way.

"I guess it comes with the territory," he says. "My parents always encouraged us to express ourselves creatively."

He's a child of his environment, he explains. "Oceans and mountains and rainforests—the west coast of B.C. offers a cornucopia of outdoor gifts. I mean, how can you lose around here? The thing is, though, it wasn't just the natural setting that inspired me. The human element played a big part, too. Our house was always full of creative people. Painters, writers, architects, potters—people who were successful at what they did. But not just in a monetary sense. But in a creative way, too."

Consider his own house. "I guess you could say it was a family project," says Massey proudly. A quirky—but very effective—West Coast Modernist take on mountain living, the three-story wooden-beam and glass structure boasts some of the best views in the Whistler Valley. And it's comfortable, too. The house is ultimately functional: open, with big, high ceilings—a perfect party house. Yet it's also blessed with private nooks and hidden crannies that add vastly to its charm. It was designed by his famous-architect father, Geoff. It was built—over a 10-year span—by Binty, his wife, Cheryl, and a posse of friends.

Binty in his graffiti-artist days. His family was one of the first to build a winter home at Whistler.

"It was guerilla house-building at its best," explains Binty. "A bunch of us were all building at the same time. So we'd simply swap work hours. If someone put 30 hours into my place, the next week—or the next week, or the next week after that—I'd put 30 hours of work into his place." He smiles. "And in that way, we were all able to afford to build here. After all, if you're not creative with how you spend your money at Whistler, you soon won't have much left to work with."

While Canada doesn't really have any equivalent to the famous dynasties like the Rockefellers or Kennedys of the United States, the Massey family comes close. Considered one of the country's most powerful families in the late 19th and early 20th centuries, the straitlaced Masseys of southern Ontario were hardworking entrepreneurs who parlayed a farm-implement business into a multimillion-dollar manufacturing empire.

And while little of that fortune managed to trickle down to the Masseys' modern-day descendants, Binty's physical profile does indeed harken back to his prominent forebears. He has the same rapier nose and high forehead that his actor-grandfather, Raymond Massey, made famous on the Broadway stage and Hollywood screen 60 years ago. The same sharply defined cheekbones that his great-uncle, Vincent Massey (the first Canadian-born Governor General of Canada), displayed during the opening and closing of parliament in 1950s. But he's different, too. More relaxed-looking. Looser. More West Coast.

The artwork displayed in his house, for example, is an unpretentious tribute to his family's talents. Among the many pieces of his own pottery lining the walls—very Asian in conception, or Nouveau Pacific, if you like—are delicately wrought baskets, bowls and hats that his wife, Cheryl, weaves from cedar bark in the traditional native manner. The lightness of their designs nicely offsets Binty's very masculine ceramic style. On the walls are his artist-mother's paintings—fine-brushed landscapes of West Coast ocean scenes. His sister's photography is everywhere.

"It's really great," says Binty. "Now that I've built a gallery in the backyard, I can sell Mom's works, Cheryl's works and my own stuff all at the same time. And they all complement each other nicely." He smiles. "That's another great thing about living at Whistler. Other artists have to go to craft fairs and Christmas fairs to sell their wares. But not me. I've got two million tourists wandering around the valley looking for something special to buy." And he smiles. "And the funny thing is: There's no competition!"

But it even goes further than that. Living at Whistler, maintains Binty, answers all the needs of his profession. "As an artist," he says, "I need a workplace where I can be quiet and focused on my art. And this is definitely a hard place to beat for that. Yet it's busy enough now that people are buying our stuff year-round." It doesn't hurt either, that Binty's distinctive ceramic works are featured at some of the most prestigious restaurants at Whistler. "The word is getting out, for sure. We're getting a lot more referrals than we ever had before."

Still, argues Binty, the most important reason he lives at Whistler is for the bounty of outdoor activities the valley offers. "How can I lose? In my front yard is the best skiing and snowboarding in North America. In my backyard is the best mountain biking. I can jump on my snowmobile and be riding on the Pemberton Icecap in a matter of minutes. I can drive down-valley and be wind-surfing within an hour. In fact, at Whistler, I can ski, ride and windsurf all in the same day. And that's something you can't say about a lot of places."

That's why, he says, the original decision to move up to Whistler full-time was so easy. At least at first.

"The last couple years of school were tough to get through, particularly in the winter," he admits. By grade 12, he was extending his Whistler weekends from Thursday night to Tuesday morning. And his parents weren't impressed.

"The minute I graduated from high school, I had my bags packed and I was headed north. My older brother, Raymond, had moved up here two years before. So it was pretty easy for me to fit in. My parents, however, kept insisting that I should continue my schooling."

It was the summer of 1976 and a new sport was being introduced to the valley. "That was the summer," remembers Massey, "that I learned to windsurf on Alta Lake—at the legendary Mt. Whistler Lodge—naked." When the laughter subsides, he continues. "It may sound like a cliché, but that was exactly the way it was."

And he's quite right. For in many ways, the mid '70s was Whistler's golden era. Like the pot of gold at the end of the rainbow, Whistler, by this point, had become this magical, legendary place for young Canadians looking to escape the humdrum existence of middle-class suburban life. Everything was permitted in those years. Nudity, drugs, communal-life experiments and skiing your buns off from dawn till dusk. It was the era of the UIC Ski Team, the Magic Mushroom Society and the Freakers' Ball. For those of us who first settled in the valley during this period, it was a life-changing experience.

Granted, there was still very little commercial development in the valley. If you had to go to the bank or had laundry to do—or even if you wanted groceries—you had to travel 40 miles down-valley and do it in Squamish. As for lodging, things were tight. Unless you had connections—or were willing to bunk out in very limited surroundings—you were out of luck. But that was a big part of the valley's charm, too.

"Everyone kind of looked out for everyone else during those years," says Binty. "It was like a big tribe."

The mountain was ours. Especially midweek, when Whistler would be transformed into an empty, slumbering giant. And we took full advantage of it.

"I don't think I've ever skied as hard or as passionately as I did during my first full winter at Whistler," says Massey. "I think it might have been the happiest time of my life."

What was really surprising to me during those years was just how unknown Whistler was outside a very small group of aficionados. Everywhere I traveled (and I traveled a lot in those days), I waxed eloquent on Whistler's special gifts: How you could climb to Whistler Peak and

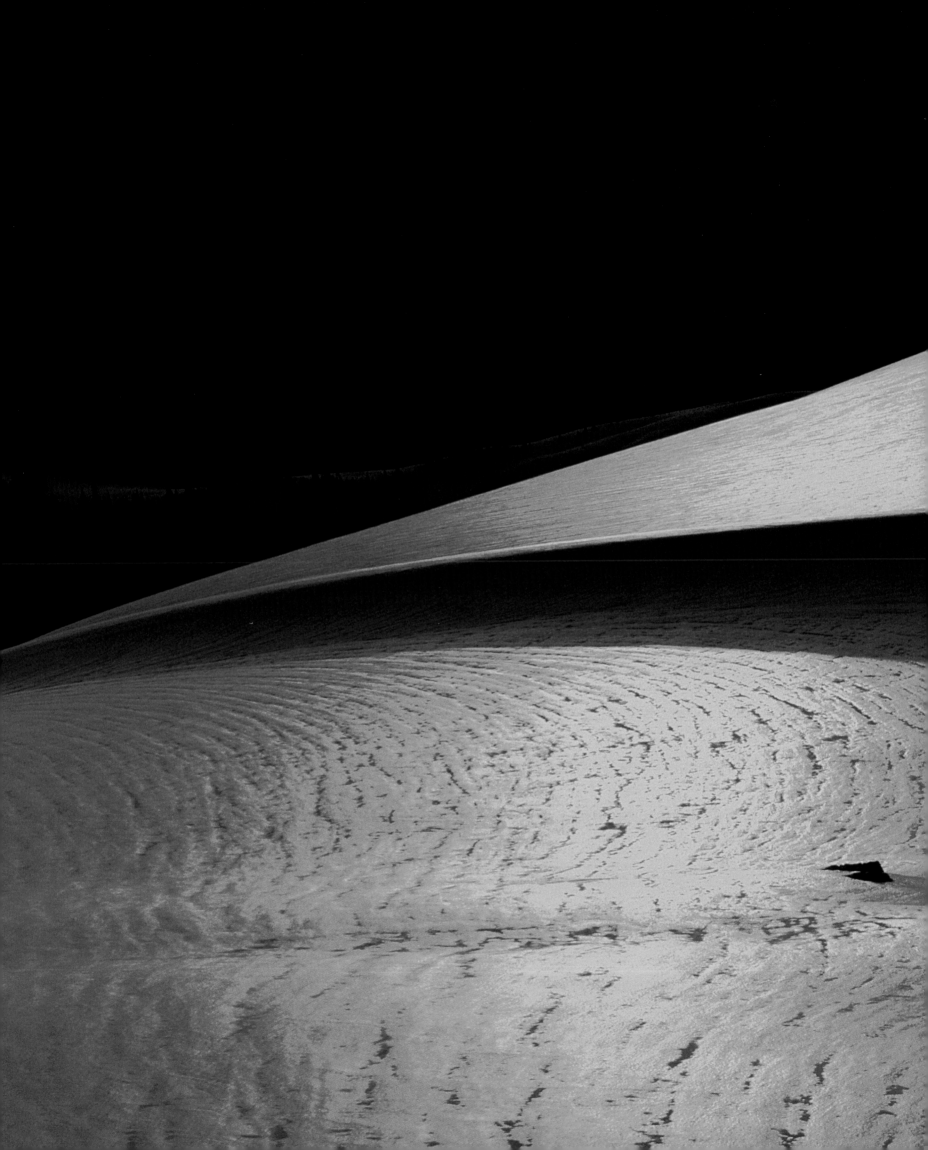

Sunrise above Rainbow Mountain.

Ski touring above the mist.

After the Storm: Morning light shines on Chateau Whistler.

The situation was tense. Bankruptcies, unemployment and broken contracts littered the way. The new village site was a mess of unfinished buildings and abandoned construction sites.

"It certainly didn't look pretty," says Drew Meredith. A young realtor in the early 1980s—and president of the Whistler Resort Association—Meredith admits he considered leaving the valley more than once during those years. "There was no momentum. It just wasn't happening. Blackcomb wasn't moving. Whistler wasn't moving. And real estate was in the toilet."

That's when the B.C. government finally decided to intervene. On January 3, 1983, the provincial government announced that it had formed a new company, WLC Developments, to take over the assets and liabilities of the struggling Whistler Village Land Company (WVLC), which for all intents and purposes had gone bankrupt. And while the decision drew howls of outrage from taxpayers across the province—local media labeled it "a bailout for the rich"—John Johnston, the deputy minister of B.C.'s Ministry of Lands, Parks and Housing, defended the deal aggressively. "Whistler does create jobs, it does create revenue," said Johnston. "We think Whistler has a good multiplier effect."

"You could almost hear the sigh of relief that went up from local business people," says Meredith. "Although the price of getting Whistler out of its quagmire of debt was high, it was our only chance of salvation at the time."

And the deal was indeed harsh. For while the government secured a $21 million loan for the ailing resort, it also removed the decision-making process from local hands. "Suddenly we were at the mercy of directors appointed to the board of WLC Developments," says Meredith. "And none of them really knew anything about running—or developing—a modern mountain resort."

In 1985, Meredith lost his patience. "I was thoroughly pissed off," he admits. "The Municipal Council of the day was awash in the 'me, me, me' syndrome. And WLC Developments was being run by guys with a 'shopping center' mentality. Against all my better instincts—I decided to run for mayor."

He won the '86 election by a landslide.

Meredith had a clear agenda. "I wanted to get the government off our backs," he says. And his timing couldn't have been better. "Although I didn't realize it at the time," he explains, "[Vancouver's] Expo '86 played a huge role in our recovery." It was the official coming-out party for the young metropolis. And with its growing reputation as an international destination came a greater awareness of the world-class mountain playground located in its backyard.

"Aspen's sale of Blackcomb Mountain was huge for us, too," says Meredith, "The whole vision changed. Intrawest said 'world-class' all the way."

The final piece of the puzzle, he says, was when CP Hotels announced that it was building one of its landmark Chateaux at the base of Blackcomb. "That's when we were finally able to get into the summer game. Up until that point, we were strictly a winter destination. But with the arrival of Chateau Whistler came the need for developing summer amenities—municipal parks, trails and lake access. Before 1986, the municipality didn't even have a parks department. And we knew at once that had to change."

But the municipality wasn't big enough yet to generate the kind of tax revenue for such ancillary services as parks and public beaches. So Meredith and his council cohorts came up with a plan.

"We put this multimedia presentation together—called "Whistler Inc.: A Case Study of an Exceptional Enterprise"—in order to convince the government to allow us to impose a special resort-wide sales tax. Our message was simple: We can't support the resort, in the quality the people expect, based on the existing municipal tax regime."

And for once the government listened. It legislated a new two percent hotel sales tax for Whistler, which ultimately paved the way for its future growth. "It's one of the accomplishments I'm most proud of," says Meredith. "That tax now generates four to five million dollars annually for the municipality."

Whistler was finally getting back on its feet. By the early 1990s, the new Village North site was in full expansion, and WLC Developments had finally recovered the money it had put up 10 years before. In fact, the B.C. government had turned quite a profit on its investment. It was time for the government to loosen its noose around Whistler's neck. Which it did in 1995, when Municipal Affairs Minister Darlene Marzari announced that the Resort Municipality of Whistler would once again be allowed to pass its own bylaws.

"The government got its money back—and then some," concludes Meredith, who stepped down from office in 1990 after a second (unopposed) term as mayor. "And they got this amazing renewable resource that has been pouring tax revenue into its coffers ever since." He laughs. "It was a win-win deal all around."

be virtually assured of a 5,000-foot powder run from summit to valley. How the snow fell straight down from December until May. How those primordial red cedars and grandfather firs made you feel so tiny as you wound your way between them in bottomless fluff.

Mostly I was greeted with dumb looks—particularly in the United States. Whistler? British Columbia? Isn't that somewhere in South America near Venezuela? I couldn't believe how ignorant people were. Especially since it was so clear to me that there was something pretty special going on with the young people living at Whistler in those years.

"There was this culture, this lifestyle, at the time that was very appealing," explains Massey. "Guys like Charlie Doyle, Andy Munster, Dave Murray—they were a lot older than me, but they were still very cool. And very creative. I don't know why exactly, but there were a lot of very interesting people living here at that time."

For many of us during those years, life came down to a simple equation. Work hard enough during the summer—at construction or tree planting or commercial fishing or mining—to pay for your season pass and your winter's rent up front. "Then," recalls Binty, "all you had to worry about was scrounging up enough money during the winter for food and beer."

But that wasn't good enough for Binty's parents.

"There had always been this underlying assumption in my family that we would all pursue post-secondary educations," he recalls. "And my parents kept pestering me about returning to school."

So he did.

"I had gotten hooked on making pots during my last few years in high school. So I decided: 'What the heck. If I'm going back to school, I might as well go learn something interesting.'"

Out of the blue he applied to the prestigious West Surrey College of Art in England.

"Imagine my surprise," he says, "when I found out I was accepted."

But Binty wasn't quite ready to leave Whistler yet.

"I only lasted one year in England," he recalls. "I came back to Whistler with my tail between my legs and spent another winter on the mountain. But it was such a bad snow year that I was eventually convinced to go back to England and finish my degree."

He says he's only now appreciating how important that time away from Whistler was for his career: "The only reason I was able to stick to my studies and finally

get my ceramics degree was because of the lack of distractions. Sure, I traveled to the Alps every Christmas for a ski holiday. But on a day-to-day basis, I was able to immerse myself in my studies in a way I could have never done if I'd tried to do the same thing in Vancouver."

"After all," he says with a grin, "how long could I have focused on my studies with Whistler just up the road?"

By 1982, he was back in B.C. with his newly minted bachelor of arts degree, making pots in a small studio he'd built on his parents' property just outside of Horseshoe Bay. "I just didn't want to go back to Whistler and fall back into the same old lifestyle," explains Binty. "But I could still feel its tug."

"I met him soon after that," says his spouse of 17 years, Cheryl Saunders Massey. A model and aspiring actress, she was introduced to the young potter by a mutual friend.

"He was pretty high on himself in those days," she remembers. "Living at his parents waterfront home—fishing, water-skiing and windsurfing every day. Basically just hanging out and doing nothing. It looked like a lot of fun. And I thought to myself: 'Hey, I want in on this.'"

Soon the two were an item. By the time 1985 rolled around, the couple was expecting their first baby. "That was definitely a big year for us," admits Binty. "We bought a dog. Got pregnant. Bought a lot at Whistler. Got married. Built a house..."

Fortunately for the young couple, lots were still relatively cheap in 1985. While the B.C. economy had already begun to inch its way back up to pre-recession levels, the real-estate market at Whistler was still struggling to reestablish itself after the disaster of '81–'82.

"We had quite a selection of lots to choose from," says Binty. "And the one we finally picked was still pretty reasonably priced—only $40,000." Harnessing his father's architectural expertise to nail down the design and using the help of friends and neighbors to offset the labor costs, Binty was able to build his house for a fraction of the normal construction price. "It couldn't have happened any other way," he says. "We simply didn't have the money."

Binty's son, Tyler, was born later that year. Michaele, his daughter, came along in 1988.

"Whistler's been a good place to bring up kids," he says. "It's a pretty tightly knit community. Everybody knows everybody else. It's not perfect, of course. But generally, the kids have enjoyed growing up here."

Like so many other people at Whistler, the Masseys

Binty and wife Cheryl in their backyard gallery. For the Masseys, creating art is a family affair.

have never shied away from getting involved in community projects. Whether serving on an arts-and-tourism board for the municipality or setting up a new off-road cycling association to manage Whistler's burgeoning mountain-bike scene, cutting new riding trails on the mountain or donating pots for a local charity fundraiser, Binty can always be trusted to be in the thick of things. "I like to get in there and get things done. There are a lot of talkers in this community. Fortunately, there are a lot of doers, too."

Take Whistler's legendary Search and Rescue (SAR) Team. While the terrain around Whistler offers up some of the best conditions in the world for big-mountain skiing and snowboarding, it can also create some of the most intimidating conditions for those who venture beyond the boundary ropes and get lost. Barely a week goes by in the year when the Search and Rescue Team isn't called out to find yet another misplaced snowboarder, skier, snowshoer or even hiker. "It's a tough job, no question about it," says Binty. "And it can get scary as hell. But it's one of the most exciting jobs I've ever been involved with."

His involvement with the program began 12 years ago, when his neighbor Dave Cathers, who was the head of the valley's Search and Rescue Team at the time, asked him to help on a very technical search on nearby Sproat Mountain. "I didn't have all the credentials and such," says Binty, "and I was definitely not a mountain climber. But I'd been a bushwhacker all my life. I figured, at the very least, that I had accumulated a little knowledge about the backcountry during that time. So I decided to pitch in and do what I could to help with the search."

That first rescue effort proved to be something of a life-changing experience for Massey. "I was quite moved by the whole process. So I decided to join the team." He pauses. Tries to find the right words. "As stressful as it can be—as dangerous as it is too often—it's been a very gratifying relationship for me. As much as I've put in, I've gotten at least as much back. People keep asking me: 'Do you guys get paid for this?' And when I tell them it's all volunteer work, they always seem surprised. But I've learned so much. I've taken all sorts of courses: rope rescue, water rescue, first aid, tracking, map work—you name it, I've studied it."

"Besides," he says "it's kind of neat to get involved with a group of guys I didn't really know and realize we all share the same passions. After all, it only takes one rescue to hammer home how important our role is."

A major turning point for the Whistler Search and Rescue program came with the tragic death of Anne Marie Potton, a young local woman who disappeared on Whistler Mountain during a hike in October 1994. Despite a weeklong search effort by more than 150 volunteers—supported by helicopters, dogs and heat-seeking sensors—she wasn't found until the next September.

"We couldn't believe how close the search parties had come to finding her when we finally found her body," says Binty. "We also realized just how important an early search is in cases like this."

Nobody knows exactly what happened on the afternoon of October 10. But evidence suggests that Potton apparently slipped on the slick glacial ice while trying to climb down Whistler Bowl late in the afternoon, broke her leg in the subsequent fall, and died of exposure before the search for her had even begun. An early October storm had covered her body with rain and then snow, and she'd literally melted into the glacier overnight. "That's why the dogs couldn't smell her," explains Massey. "In essence, the snow and rain had sealed her into the mountain."

The SAR Team learned an awful lot during that week, says Binty. "All of a sudden, we were leading people who really didn't know what they were doing. And it was up to us to shape our different teams into an effective unit. It made us realize just how important our training was."

Of greater importance however, was the amount of media attention that the Whistler Search and Rescue program got during the protracted search.

"I think a lot of local people took the program for granted before Anne Marie's death," opines Massey. "But they certainly got a wake-up call after that. We raised a heck of a lot of money due to that search." He pauses. Shakes his head. "Before Anne Marie, we had nothing. In fact, we were each responsible for providing our own safety gear. All that's changed now. Today the Whistler SAR has a huge equipment room...and a much higher profile."

"Where do you wanna go?" asks Binty Massey. It's snowing hard now. Big, thick flakes that plaster themselves against our goggles. The wind howls menacingly through the alpine scrub around us. The storm is at its peak.

"Not sure," I tell him. Below us is over 4,000 vertical feet of Coast Mountain forest. Four thousand vertical feet of trackless snow. "I think I'm gonna explore the right gully this time," I add. "Haven't been there in a while, and I'd kinda like to check it out." I know it's going to be good there. Deep. "See you in the clearing?"

He nods. "See you in the clearing."

And we push off together into a cloud of bottomless turns. One, two, three big arcs. Already we're flying. Suddenly Binty peels off sharply to the left and drops into his favorite chute. He disappears behind a veil of falling snow.

I'm all alone—floating effortlessly over what is usually an ugly, impassable band of rocks. Steep, really steep. And so much snow—it's almost unbelievable how much snow there is. Yet I'm still riding near the surface, the broad contours of my board still visible between turns. One quick slash. Drive the board across the fall line. A little air between turns. Then another slash. Suddenly the snow starts to move. Look sharp. I plane over the sluff's bow wave and power-cruise into the gully below.

Yeahoo! Powder Super G.

I'm now in the thick of it. The belly of the gully is as full as I've ever seen it, and I'm hard pressed to keep from stalling. Waves of white flow over my head. Big clumps stick to my goggles. Get in my nostrils. Plug up my mouth. I snort, and choke in a snow-filled breath of air. Cough out the snow and try to snag some oxygen.

But still I keep my board pointed downhill. Can't slow down now. Gotta keep the momentum going. Speed is my friend.

The narrowest, steepest section of the gully is just ahead. The snow is lighter here. More powdery. I drive my board straight up the right wall. *Now!* Pop off a little stump and free-fall back down into a thick mattress of untracked snow. *Oooh.* Now a big drawn-out bottom turn—heavy g's—and a rail-ride back up to the rim. I drag my hand along the bank just 'cuz it feels so good.

Like a frozen wave, only softer and silkier than the summer version.

Eventually the gully spits me out into a forest of grandfather fir and cedar—first growth. Never seen an axe or a chainsaw. The snow is soft here, and I let my board fly where it will.

There is so much new snow that the underbrush is now fully covered. It's just me and the big trees. Riding at its most magnificent. I pat the back of a gnarly old Douglas fir as I go by, its thick ridged bark a testament to its longevity, pop off a recent windfall and float into the next turn.

Another day. Another powder session.

Aaaah. So smooth. So natural.

Suddenly, to my left, I spot Binty's fleeting silhouette. He's about 50 feet over, following almost the same line I am through the trees. A big rooster tail of snow rises behind his every turn. Hangs in the air for just a moment before floating lazily back down to the ground. It looks splendid in the late afternoon light.

But I can't get stuck on watching Binty. There's still lots of vertical left. And a couple of tight little sections just ahead.

By the time we reach the clearing, it's nearly dark. We still have a long, slow slog ahead of us, but the ride down was worth it. In spades.

"Can you believe how deep it was in the upper chutes?" enthuses Binty. He is still buzzing. And grinning from ear to ear. "There must have been three, four feet of new. Easy."

I nod in agreement. "Yeah. Nice to share it with you, pal."

He sighs. "Too bad somebody had to die to make it happen."

But Binty is never one to dwell too long on the negatives. Not even when it concerns him directly. Diagnosed with cancer in the fall of 2000—Hodgkin's disease, to be precise—he spent nearly a year fighting the disease. And he did it with everything at his disposal. Yoga, visualization, holistic medicine and finally, when he'd run out of other options, chemotherapy. He lost his hair, lost his muscles and got weaker and weaker. For a while, all he could do was lie on the couch and stare out his window at Whistler and Blackcomb. But he never gave up. Nor did he ever get down.

"It was a very tough period in our lives," admits Cheryl, who stood by her man every step of the way. "But we just figured we would get through it come what may."

Laughs Binty: "It's not like you're going to give up and just die. You have to find a way to get through it. And we did."

Today, the cancer is in remission. Call it luck. Or the power of positive thinking. Or simply the power of good drugs. Whatever. Binty is back at work in his studio behind the house making pots. He's also snowboarding again and mountain biking and windsurfing—and even snowmobiling. "Did [the cancer] change me? I don't think so. I know I appreciate the little things more now. But I've always been blessed with a pretty large love of life."

He smiles. Outside the clouds are lifting. A late-afternoon sun is bathing Blackcomb Mountain in a warm wash of reds and oranges. The Masseys' living room now feels cozier than ever. "You know," says Binty, as he pours us each one last cup of tea, "I think it's that same love of life that got me through my cancer." He pauses for a moment. Smiles again. "That, and of course, all the love and support I got from my friends and family. For without them, I'd be nothing."

Above: **Binty beachcombing on B.C.'s West Coast. A child of his surroundings, Binty is a man for all seasons.**
Opposite: **For many Whistler residents, life is all about striking the right balance between work, play and more play.**

CHAPTER 7
CATHY JEWETT

It is still dark outside. And very quiet. Moon shadows dance beside us. "This is the magical part of the job for me," says Cathy Jewett, as she carefully leads our team along the exposed west rib of Whistler Peak. "It's all there, right in front of you—no excuses, no bull." She pauses for a moment. Checks the snow stability ahead. Then she starts moving again. "Our task this morning is simple," she says. "We've got to make the area safe for the skiing public. That's all."

The synchronous calls of our avalanche transceivers cut through the night air like electro-bugs on a summer evening. *Bleep. Bleep-Bleep. Bleep. Bleep-Bleep.* Our skis make a soft swishing noise as they slide over the snow.

Far away to the east, a thin sliver of light cuts across the horizon. "Looks like a great morning for dropping bombs," says Ian Bunbury, Jewett's route partner. Between them, the two Whistler patrollers carry a dozen sticks of high-powered explosives. Over the next hour, all of them will be detonated.

Nearly 15 centimeters of new snow have fallen overnight. It's not much for Whistler, but combined with the high winds that accompanied the storm, the potential for slides to occur on lee slopes this morning is fairly high—especially where we're going. And that's why we're going there. Essentially, our task is to accelerate that process.

The light quietly brings definition to our environment. Ice, snow and rock. And more rock. And more snow and ice. Directly below us is nothing. A convex slope drops blindly over a 300-vertical-foot cliff. Beyond that is a big wide-open bowl—a catcher's mitt for the monster avalanches that have ravaged this face forever. And then the forest starts.

Tiny balls of adrenaline ping across the walls of my stomach. I feel like a little kid. Something about high explosives and exposed slopes, I suppose. And the special nature of this outing, of course. The new year is

barely a few hours old—indeed, people are still partying in the valley—and I'm way up high on the mountain doing avalanche control with Whistler's pro ski patrol. It's a fitting start to the year, I figure.

"We're almost at our first bomb site," says Jewett. We stop just above a treacherous piece of terrain called the Hanging Roll—a wind-created wave of snow that is as unpredictable as it is dangerous. "Stand back behind those rocks," she instructs me. "You should get a good view from there, if anything pulls out."

She takes a few more steps forward and then stops and unslings her pack. She pulls out a stick of dynamite, inserts a long fuse and tapes it down expertly in a few wraps, reaches into her pocket for an igniter and sets it on the fuse as well. She then puts the stick between her legs, takes a quick tug and the fuse begins to smoke. She's got two and a half minutes. She takes a few practice swings—one-two-three—and then in a much-rehearsed move, she sends the stick cartwheeling end over end toward the critical edge of the drop-off. It hits, slides for a bit and then buries itself in the snow.

Jewett casually slides back to our position. Bunbury adjusts his ear guards. "One minute left," says Jewett. "It doesn't look like we should pull much out of here,"

Above: **Dan Treadway takes the straight way down. Whistler/Blackcomb's** reputation as the center of the freeride universe has a lot to do with the groundbreaking work of its mountain pro patrol. Opposite: **Cathy tossing bombs. It didn't take her long to decide what she wanted to be at Whistler. It just took her a while to break into the "old boy" confederacy.**

ERIC AND TREVOR

They were two unlikely partners. Trevor Petersen, the older one, was from urban North Vancouver—a pony-tailed, fast-talking, fast-thinking self-promoter with a thousand different ideas and too little time to do them all. Eric Pehota, the younger one, was from the northern B.C. town of Mackenzie—a heavy-eyed, slow-talking tough guy who never really let you know what he was thinking. But they both loved skiing, and they both loved mountains.

"Pehota and Petersen were perfect partners," insists Whistler photographer Paul Morrison. "Trevor was the charismatic one, while Eric was the quiet buddy. They didn't do show-off, lift-oriented stuff—it was the real deal."

They met at Apex Mountain Resort, in the interior of B.C., in the early '80s. But Apex was just too small for the two budding adventurers, and by 1984 they'd

Trevor Petersen, left, Eric Pehota.

moved to Whistler. "It was a bit of a shock at first," admits Pehota. "I hadn't really traveled a lot—I didn't make it to Vancouver until my late teens—and Whistler seemed pretty big and fancy."

But the two young men thrived. They didn't follow the big-air, big-attitude American "extreme skier" mode (think Glen Plake) that everyone was emulating during those years. Rather, they were drawn to the self-propelled, big-mountain climbing-and-skiing genre—true extreme skiing, some would say—that Trevor had encountered on an extended stay in the French Alps earlier in the decade.

By 1987, the two were beginning to attract attention. Pehota's first descent of the northwest summit of Mt. Waddington (B.C.'s highest mountain) that year, followed by a bold ascent and first descent of Dalton Dome in 1988 and, accompanied by Petersen, a daring first down Mt. Fitzsimmons in 1989, was enough to impress even the most skeptical of alpine purists.

Soon, Petersen and Pehota were posing for the magazines. With photog-

raphers like Paul Morrison and Scott Markewitz using both men as principal talent, the two young skiers suddenly found themselves as poster boys for the new Whistler ski scene. "Sure, it was exciting," drawls Pehota. "But I never took it that seriously. That was more Trevor's scene. He was more the businessman. I just wanted to go skiing."

And ski they did. As principal talent for James Angroves' RAP Entertainment, they began to travel the globe in search of the ultimate descent. And then they found Alaska's Chugach Mountains.

"Here were all these major ramps—and covered with so much snow. It was the most amazing alpine playground I'd ever encountered," says Pehota. "And virtually everything was a first descent!"

It was in the Chugach that they notched some of their most famous big-mountain runs. From the harrowingly steep slopes of Meteorite to the Eiger-like Pontoon Peak, Pehota and Petersen weren't afraid to step out and test themselves on slopes that others thought were impossible to ski. Still, they weren't getting the kind of attention their American peers were getting. And far fewer dollars were coming their way. While it frustrated Petersen no end, it didn't seem to bother Pehota all that much.

"I've never been in it for the money," Pehota explains. "To me, it's all about exploring personal limits. As far as trying to make a living from it—well, that can be pretty limiting."

Besides, things were changing for the two men. Both were married by the mid '90s, and Trevor was the father of two kids (Kye and Neve). They'd already planned to phase down their adventures. They were ready for other things.

Then tragedy hit. In February 1996, while skiing alone on one of the high couloirs in Chamonix, France, Petersen was hit by an avalanche and killed instantly. The Whistler community went into shock. Eric Pehota was devastated.

But time tends to heal all wounds, no matter how deep they cut. Today, Eric Pehota is the doting father of two boys, Logan and Dalton. Like his friend Rob Boyd, he is a founding member of the Whistler Freeride Team, and spends much of the winter working with visiting media and VIPs. As for his thirst for adventure, it is far from quenched.

In the spring of 1999, he managed a feat he'd been planning for more than 10 years—the first descent of Mt. Tantalus, a razor-sharp peak to the south of Whistler where any error on his part would have resulted in instant death. "I have dreams, I have plans," he explains. "They are always there. I just don't talk about them a lot."

Above Right: **The boys at the office.**
Below Right: **Long walks and hairy climbs were all part of the fun.**

she tells me confidently. Then she smiles. "But ya never know." Thirty seconds. Fifteen. Ten. "Cover your ears, it's going to be loud!" *BLAM*. The earth shakes.

Suddenly a fracture cuts across where Jewett was standing only a few minutes before, and a massive slab of snow detaches itself from the slopes. Clouds of white lift high into the air as the slab drops out of sight. The mountain roars. "Wow," mouths Cathy.

A few seconds later, a thick tongue of snow reappears a thousand feet below. Moving fast—expending its energy in the bowl. From here it looks benign. Almost inconsequential. But we all know it could easily swallow a person. Kill one, even.

"Well, I was wrong about that one," says Jewett, still smiling. "Let's go on to the next site and see what kind of action we can find there."

Below us are clouds. Lots of them. Like fingers of a roiling tide, they fill the valleys almost to timberline. Only the highest summits—Rainbow across the valley, the Black Tusk to the south, and the great Tantalus Massif near the coast—manage to thrust their snouts above the gray flood. Where we are standing, however, is perfectly clear. In fact, the sun is just beginning to make its way over the horizon just behind Overlord Mountain.

It feels like I'm in a dream.

"Beautiful, isn't it?" asks Jewett. I nod. "I never get tired of the early morning light here," she adds. "It's what makes me come back to this job season after season."

A 20-year veteran of the Whistler Mountain patrol—and the mother of two children—Jewett is an old hand at this. One of the first female pro patrollers to be hired by Whistler Mountain after the north-side expansion in 1980, the former liftie they called "Pusscakes" (from the *Penthouse* cartoon "Wicked Wanda") has pretty much seen it all.

"It's like being part of a big family," she explains. And then she smiles. "How can I put this? It's like having dozens of rambunctious little brothers. After all, we spend all of the major holidays together: Christmas, New Year's, Easter, even. You're never alone if you're a member of the pro patrol here."

Indeed. Whistler's pro patrollers are a tribe onto themselves. And they don't like being mistaken for ski bums. They are multidisciplined paramedics who can splint a shattered femur one moment, and perform a cornice rescue the next. They are demolition experts who can pinpoint the critical section in a hanging cornice and blow it up perfectly, and child psychologists

Opposite: First tracks on Rainbow Mountain. Jewett spent most of her early years at Whistler exploring her new playground.
Below: A fisherman's wife, Cathy spent a whole summer trolling for salmon off B.C.'s wild coastline.

who can pick up a lost kid on evening sweep and keep him warm and entertained all the way to the valley. It's a career path suited to only the most committed.

And the most talented.

"On a big mountain like Whistler, patrolling is akin to the proverbial iceberg," says Jewett. "Most people barely see the tip of what we do up here. There's a lot of stress associated with this job. But then, too, there are a lot of benefits."

And she knows exactly what those are. Cathy Jewett first came to Whistler in the fall of 1976. "I moved here from Toronto with a girlfriend," she says. "We were planning to go to Banff. But we heard the skiing was way better at Whistler. So we kept going west." Places were hard to come by that year, but Jewett was lucky. "We hooked up with a bunch of guys right away," she remembers. "It was far from perfect—there were eight of us sharing a two-bedroom suite—but it worked out somehow."

By the spring of '77, the young, outgoing blond had talked herself into a job on the mountain as a lift attendant on the Alpine T-bar. There, in the shadow of Whistler Peak, she would watch Chris Stethem and John Hetherington and Roger McCarthy do their avalanche control routes early in the morning after big storms. "I came from the flatlands of Ontario," she says. "To me, being a pro patroller at Whistler seemed a terribly romantic job." So she kept watching, and learning.

Jewett says she can remember the exact day she decided to become a member of that team.

"It was March 10, 1977," she explains. "A big storm cycle had just come through, and the patrol was getting some really big results that morning. I remember a huge slide coming down Surprise. It had, at least, a three-meter fracture."

In those days, there were no alpine lifts servicing the upper mountain. From the top of the T-bars, it was a 40-minute hike, at least, to the summit of Whistler. Patrollers were often the only people allowed up there. And like patrollers all over the world, they took full advantage of their privileges. Their signature piece back then was a classic run called Shale Slope. It was there, in full view of the guests sitting in the Roundhouse Lodge, that the patrollers would show off their big-mountain skiing skills after finishing their control rounds in the high alpine.

"For Whistler patrollers, Shale Slope is Shangri-La, Valhalla and nirvana combined," explains Cathy. "And Shale looked particularly yummy that morning. So

when the guys decided to ski it without dropping a bomb into it first, I knew exactly what they were in for."

It was every patroller's dream come true, says Jewett. "I watched in amazement as they came dancing down the hill. It was face-shots at every turn. Snow going over their heads. It was magical and crazy and totally inspiring."

She stops talking for a moment. Grins that tomboy grin of hers, the one that says: "Go on. Give it your best shot. You can't scare me." It's the same damn-the-torpedoes grin that has gotten her into trouble—and then out of trouble—for most of her life.

"Well," she continues, "it was at that point that I decided what I wanted to do with myself. I'd found my life's work: Throw bombs. Ski powder. Cheat death. Save lives. And break hearts."

No matter that she had no qualifications for the job. No matter even that Whistler Mountain had never hired a women pro patroller before. Cathy Jewett had decided what she wanted. And nobody—but nobody—was going to stop her.

"That was my magic day," adds Jewett. Up until that point she was only taking a year off from life in Toronto. After March 10, her life took a whole new turn. "That was all it took. One day of sunshine, powder and big avalanches. After that, I was on a mission."

It took her nearly four years to break down Whistler's defenses. She even enrolled in nursing school at one point in a desperate bid to show management just how serious she was. But nothing worked. "It was definitely a male enclave," she says of the old-boy patrol network at Whistler. "It was almost like a secret society, in fact. You didn't get hired on as much as you got invited in."

But all that was about to change. With the development of Whistler Village in 1980, the new launch at Blackcomb Mountain and the expansion onto the north side of Whistler Mountain, well-qualified pro patrollers were soon in big demand. "They had to hire 12 new patrollers on Whistler that winter," says Jewett. "So they relented and hired three of us "weaker-sex" types—Eileen Purcell, Gail Morrison and me." The fourth woman on the patrol that year, Jan Tindle, had been hired the year before.

Whistler Mountain would never be the same again.

"The teasing was pretty intense those first years," she admits. But the women chosen to break into Whistler's patrol ranks were all very talented. "It didn't take long," says Jewett, "for the boys to realize we could

All tied up. It wasn't always easy to be a woman in a man's world. But it could be fun.

do just about anything they could. And do it better, too!"

Meanwhile, Jewett was still looking for a place at Whistler she could call her own—at least for a little while. "I remember my friend Kelly King inviting me to Christmas dinner at her mum's house one year," she explains. "It was really soon after I arrived at Whistler. Must have been 1977. Anyway, it was there that I met Myrtle Philip. And I was just thrilled to meet her and hear her story. To me, it was amazing to be talking to one of the first pioneers in this valley." She pauses. "I just couldn't imagine what it would have been like living up here in the '10s and '20s."

Although Myrtle's fabled Rainbow Lodge had burned down earlier that year, there were a number of outlying buildings on the property that were still habitable. And Cathy was intrigued enough with Myrtle and her story to look into renting one of them for herself. "It was a really funky place," she says of the rustic caretaker's cabin she moved into in 1980. "Floors going all over the place. Hand-hewn furniture made of native woods. It was a very special experience."

She lived on the Philips' former property for nearly seven years. "Living at Rainbow," she says, "was like living in the backcountry. Poorly insulated, insufficiently heated, frozen pipes, no water: It was crazy. My roommates were party animals. Their evenings would just be winding down when I was getting up for work. When I got home in the evening, they were just waking up.

"Still," she says, with more than a hint of nostalgia in her voice, "it was a great group of people to live with. Besides, given the atmosphere at Whistler in those years, it didn't seem to be that crazy of a lifestyle."

For Jewett and many skiers of her generation, the 1980s were a special time. "The tourists hadn't yet arrived in big numbers, we had these two huge mountains to play on, and we had this very cool community of like-minded mountain lovers. For me, it was a time of pure adventure. We'd just take out a map of the area and go."

Singing Pass. Fissile Peak. Overlord Glacier. Garibaldi Lake. Rainbow Mountain. The Callaghan. Wedge Mountain. Mt. Currie. She visited them all. "Those early years were all about skiing and exploring for me. In the winter, I was on my skis seven days a week. In the summer, I'd go hiking whenever I could." She stops. Chuckles at her memories. "Thinking back to the equipment we used to get around in those days—it's amazing that we're still alive. I mean, I remember coming down Singing Pass Trail wearing a huge pack on my back and skiing on narrow, wooden cross-country skis with no edges."

But there were incidents. And accidents. And Jewett had her share of close calls. "I remember one year—it was probably around 1982," says Jewett. "There was a whole gang of us in Horstman Glacier." This was still in the days before Hugh Smythe had spirited the T-bar away from Fortress Mountain and installed it in the Blackcomb high country. So skiing in the alpine there was still very much a self-propelled off-piste adventure.

She continues: "I hadn't intended to go skiing in the backcountry, so I didn't have a probe or a shovel in my pack. But everyone insisted I'd be fine, so I decided to go along anyway. I should have known better." At first, everything was fine. The climb up into the glacier went by without incident. It was on the way down that the group encountered trouble. "Despite being warned to go one at a time," says Jewett, "everyone started to bunch up and ski across a slope. I stayed in a safe spot to watch." Suddenly, the snow began to move. "And everyone but me got carried for a ride. One guy got completely buried. But I had watched him go, knew exactly where he'd disappeared, and dug him out with my hands." In an offhand tone, she admits he was totally buried, "but he was pretty close to the surface, so it wasn't that hard."

Was she scared? "I don't remember being scared. I don't even remember being particularly excited." And then, as if to explain herself. "It wasn't a particularly big avalanche. It was just big enough to bury you."

It was also during these heady mountain-adventure years that many of the off-piste classics around Whistler first earned their monikers. Like Ladies First, for example. "Back before there were lifts in Seventh Heaven," says Jewett, "we would hike up Chainsaw Ridge on a regular basis. To really push the envelope, we'd hike into Blackcomb Glacier." She giggles. "It was a pretty big adventure back in the early '80s. Basically, nobody did it."

One day in late spring, Cathy and "a bunch of the guys," she remembers, decided to climb up above the

windlip on Blackcomb Glacier, head toward Spearhead Glacier and hit the big north-facing slope beyond. "I was leaving the next day to work in the bush for the summer. So the guys said, 'ladies first,' and offered me first tracks. Well, I certainly didn't have to be asked twice, so I immediately took off. I came onto the slope with my weight too far forward, the snow broke under my tips and pitched me forward, and I rode the whole slope on my nose. You could see my fingernail marks in the snow all the way down. Talk about embarrassing."

But her reputation was already well secured. Respected for her physical strength—"I'm not that big," she says, "but I'm tough"—she was also known as someone you could count on to remain cool when things got tight. "There's not much that will faze me," she admits. "I've been through too much over the years to get into a flap during emergencies."

As far as dealing with accidents—the bane of a pro patroller's life—Jewett says she's been lucky over the past two decades. "It's just been a steady learning curve as far as first aid goes. Broken bones—the femurs are the worst—blown-out knees, head lacerations from the old runaway straps. That kind of thing." What she doesn't mention is that she's also had to deal with a number of on-hill fatalities and spinal injuries. "We try

not to dwell on that stuff," she admits.

"In the old days," she continues, "we used to have a full-time doctor on patrol. So we got really good on-hill instruction: how to suture, how to assess patients' trauma, how to reset a dislocated shoulder."

Of course, there wasn't much backup in the valley in terms of emergency care in those years. So the patrollers were often forced to use helicopters to evacuate their patients to Vancouver. "I remember flying into town with a patient, getting off the helicopter at the hospital—still in my ski boots and winter clothes—and being surrounded by people in shorts and tennis whites. Sometimes the juxtaposition of mountain and city could be quite funny."

Like most of her peers at Whistler, Cathy soon tired of not having a place that she could really call home. "Living at Rainbow was great," she says, "but I knew it wasn't a permanent arrangement. And I badly wanted my own house."

So she began spending her summers in the north to raise some home-building seed money. "I spent 10 years working in the bush—from 1980 to 1990. I worked in the Yukon and Northwest Territories, mostly. A few times in northern B.C. In logging camps, mineral explo-

Above: The remains of Rainbow Lodge. Following in the footsteps of Myrtle Philip, Cathy Jewett spent her early years at Whistler "camping" in one of the Lodge's outlying buildings. Opposite: Nick Kaulbauch sets some steep tracks off Blackcomb Peak. In the 1980s, there was so much terrain and so few skiers that getting fresh tracks was never much of an issue.

The sharp-edged teeth of Mt. Fee
rises up out of the clouds.

ration camps mostly. I was the cook and first-aid attendant. And quite often, I was the only woman." She laughs, but there's not much humor there. "It was touch and go a lot of the time," she admits. "I'm not scared of much, but there were moments where I thought I was done for."

But she never backed down. And she kept reminding herself constantly why she was putting herself through this in the first place. "I just focused on the house I was going to build for myself at Whistler. Most days it got me through."

By the late '70s, many young Whistlerites were already concerned that the hot real-estate market was quickly leaving them behind. How were they ever going to afford a home here if prices just kept going up and up? A number of different co-op development schemes were floated. And sank just as fast.

In the summer of 1980, Jewett decided to buy into a promising-looking one in a popular Whistler subdivision called Alpine Meadows. "There were 27 of us—all Whistler locals—and we bought 6.2 acres of land to develop as a strata lot. In other words, we would be communal owners of the total parcel. How we divided it up among ourselves was strictly up to us. " She pauses for

a moment. "It was a scary proposition. But I didn't have a lot of choice at the time. It was either that, or keep renting." And she'd definitely had enough of throwing her money out the window.

As it turns out, says Jewett, buying into that strata lot in Alpine Meadows was one of the best decisions in her life. "It's a really great neighborhood—really close to the wilderness, but also close to the community center and Whistler Village. For someone like myself bringing up a family at Whistler"—her son, Max, is nine, and her daughter, Bryn, is six—"this is an ideal place to live."

Building the house, however, was not so easy. "There was still a recession going on in B.C. and money was hard to come by. I'd paid cash for the house's foundation, but when it came to putting up the walls and getting a roof on, I couldn't get a mortgage."

"After all," she says, with more than a hint of sarcasm, "I was just as woman. And a woman with no permanent income to boot. I worked in the bush in the summer and worked on the hill in the winter. The bank manager just looked at me and laughed. To him, I was a risk he had no intention of taking. So it was tough."

But when Cathy Jewett sets her mind on something, she doesn't do it in half measures. "I worked damn hard to

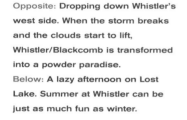

Opposite: **Dropping down Whistler's west side. When the storm breaks and the clouds start to lift, Whistler/Blackcomb is transformed into a powder paradise.**
Below: **A lazy afternoon on Lost Lake. Summer at Whistler can be just as much fun as winter.**

build that house. As soon as the mountain would close and my patrolling job was done, I'd leave directly for the bush and work seven days a week until winter came again."

And she kept this pace up for 10 years. True, she took a short trip to Nepal one year. And floated down the Colorado River another time. But mostly, Cathy kept her eyes on the prize.

"I had no choice," she says. "I needed cash."

But the house got built. And she and her kids and her husband, Jim Horner, couldn't be happier. But why wouldn't they be? The house that Cathy built is as strong and as sturdy—and as cozy and intimate—as Cathy is herself. "It turned out pretty well, I have to admit. It was hard, but it was definitely worth it."

Today, at 45, Cathy Jewett is facing another crossroads.

While a major high point in 2002 was skiing in the patrollers' torchlight parade with her son, Max, on New Year's Eve—"it's amazing how special a ritual becomes when you can also share it with your kids"—she can't help but think that her time on the mountain is slowly coming to an end. Stymied in her efforts to work her way into a management position at Whistler/Blackcomb, she has now scaled back her patrol work schedule to three days a week.

"I'm finally getting beaten down by the work," she says. "It's just not that easy anymore to spend the day toiling at such a physical job."

Yet she says she doesn't have a clue where she will direct her still-considerable energy.

"Is this the end of my ambitions on the mountain? Or just the beginning of my ambitions somewhere else? I'm not really sure right now." She stops talking. And for just a moment her eyes mist up slightly. But she quickly turns away before I can be sure of what I saw. When she turns around again, she's back in control. Back to being Cathy—practical, sensible, eminently competent Cathy.

"One of the great things about my recent shift in focus," she says, "is that I can spend more time with my kids." Another pause. Another deep breath. "And I know that something interesting will turn up for me in the meantime. It always does."

But then she gets to the nub of it. And I can feel the pain in her voice as if it were my own. "I just can't imagine—after 26 years—not working on that mountain anymore."

Above: **Cathy with children Max and Bryn. A classic overachieving mum, she continues to break new ground at Whistler.**
Opposite: **With the rigors of pro patrolling starting to take their toll, Cathy isn't sure what the future has in store for her and her family.**

CHAPTER 8
ROB BOYD

There are moments in a community's history that capture the times and the spirit of the place so well that they eventually come to define a whole era. The 1989 World Cup downhill race on Whistler Mountain was one such moment. Follow me there now. It's a good story.

Only 10 minutes left before the start of the race. Coaches, ski technicians, officials and racers all mill nervously about the enclosed space behind the Whistler Mountain start shack. Tension is high. The course is a tough one; the price of mistakes is costly here. You can almost smell the testosterone in the air.

Twenty-three-year-old Rob Boyd stands by himself near the back of the enclosure, reviewing the course in his mind.

Above: Boyd—from 2-year-old to teenager. As a kid, Boyd had the run of his father's ski area. But motorcycle racing held far more appeal than ski racing.
Opposite: Boyd and coach Terry (Toulouse) Spence ham it up for the cameras: For many Canadians, Boyd represented the face of ski racing for much of the '80s and '90s.

His eyes are closed. His long blond hair falls in loose curls at the base of his neck. He hasn't shaved all week. He looks hungry.

A couple of race volunteers ski up and nervously wish the hometown boy good luck. He looks up. Smiles. "Thanks guys," he says. "I'll be sure to give 'er my best." Then he shrugs. He doesn't know what else to say, and they stand around for a few seconds, unsure of what to do next. Finally the two fans pat him on the shoulder reassuringly, utter a couple of "We're with ya, Rob," and push off toward the course.

Boyd takes off his warm-up suit, places a pair of headphones over his ears and begins his prerace routine. He does a few neck rotations, then twists his upper body back and forth a few times. He closes his eyes, breathes deeply. He is a big man for a ski racer—over six feet two and powerfully built. In his Lycra downhill suit he looks a bit like a Marvel Comics hero. All he needs is a cape.

"WELCOME EVERYONE TO WHISTLER MOUNTAIN," squawks the race announcer through the on-hill PA system. "AND A SPECIAL WELCOME TO THE 1989 MOLSON WORLD DOWNHILL, THE LAST SPEED EVENT ON THE WORLD CUP CIRCUIT THIS YEAR."

The crowd roars its approval. Throngs of skiers line both sides of the course for nearly 3,000 vertical feet—from the start of the Dave Murray Downhill Course all the way to the finish. Aficionados mostly. From Whistler and Vancouver, mainly. And they've all got it bad this year. Whistler World Cup fever, they call it. When the weather gods smile and the snow is good and hard. When world-class athletes confront a world-class course.

It only happens once every few seasons. And even then, it's never a sure thing. After all, holding a World Cup downhill at Whistler seems somewhat counterintuitive given the resort's reputation for big storms and deep snow.

But the course itself is so exciting to ski—the path it takes down the mountain so natural—that it is considered by many racers to be one of the most challenging downhills in the world. It has a sampling of everything: speed, big air, crushing compressions, nasty transitions—it doesn't relent from start to finish. And it never lets you off easily.

Maybe that's why it has such a huge following here. Passionate, enthusiastic, supportive, knowledgeable—even verging on obsessed—Whistler downhill fans are legendary on the World Cup circuit. And this year, they definitely have someone to cheer for. Waves

Good technique, a love of speed, and an easy-going demeanor, carried Boyd to the top of the World Cup downhill hierarchy.

of excitement roll up the course as the first forerunner flashes by. The crowd is in high gear now.

Boyd turns up the volume on his Walkman. The powerful reggae beat of Alpha Blondie pulses in his head, drowning out the scattered puddles of noise, soothing him. He bends impossibly low, touches his head to his knees, stays there for a few seconds and straightens up again.

He feels strong. Already, he has two training-run victories this week. And just a few minutes ago he had the powder run of his life. While warming up, if you can believe it. Right off the Peak Chair, too. What a great omen, he thinks.

The first racer is in the start gate. Boyd gets back to business. He squats, stretches his left leg out to the side, and bends his upper body towards it. He takes a few deep breaths and drops his head down as low as it will go.

From deep inside the start hut comes a familiar voice. "Okay, Robbie," calls out Terry "Toulouse" Spence, the team's legendary trainer. "Just a few more guys before you're up. Get ready." Boyd gets up, stretches and grabs his skis from the snow. He snatches up his helmet and his poles as well, and slowly heads toward the hut.

"How ya feelin', boy?" Spense asks as Boyd slides into the start shack. A longtime Whistlerite—and a 10-year veteran of the downhill wars—Toulouse knows exactly what's at stake here for his young charge.

Boyd smiles. "I feel good. I feel really good." His mind is wrapping itself around the task ahead—his vision tunneling in on the perfect line down the course. From here on, nothing else matters.

Spence concentrates on relaxing Boyd's calves and hamstrings. He rubs steadily while he talks. "When you leave this start shack," he whispers, "you're going to hear the biggest roar you ever heard in your life." Boyd nods and takes a few more deep breaths. "Your job, my friend," says Toulouse still rubbing, "is to take that roar and make it work for you all the way down the course." He stops talking for a second. Smacks Boyd on the ass. "Know what I mean?" The starter beckons. Boyd smiles down at Spence, winks, and slides into the start gate.

"Racer ready?" The starter drops a hand on Boyd's shoulder. He nods, his eyes focused on the first set of gates 30 meters down the hill. The start sequence begins: "Three, two, one—*Beep. Beep. Beep!*"

Boyd explodes from the start hut. And hears the crowd for just a moment. Like the roar of a train, it rumbles down the course ahead of him. Then he shuts

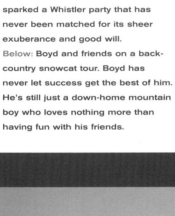

Opposite: Smiling for the hometown crowd, 1989. Boyd's downhill victory sparked a Whistler party that has never been matched for its sheer exuberance and good will.
Below: Boyd and friends on a back-country snowcat tour. Boyd has never let success get the best of him. He's still just a down-home mountain boy who loves nothing more than having fun with his friends.

S ki racing ruled supreme at Whistler in the mid 1980s. From club racing to adult racing—from 10-year-olds to 70-year-olds—everyone, it
seemed at the time, was keen on learning how to run gates. And that
enthusiasm, in large part, was due to the vision and drive of Whistler's earliest homegrown ski racing star: Dave Murray.

A charter member of the Crazy Canucks—the now-legendary group of brash
Canadian downhillers who first imposed themselves on the World Cup circuit
in the mid 1970s—Murray was the embodiment of the laid-back West Coast athlete. With his long blond hair, his guitar-playing and windsurfing, Murray sometimes acted more like a beach bum than a ski racer. But get him on a downhill
course and the easy-going hipster would turn into a hard-charging dragster.
Although he never had the good fortune of standing on the top step of the World
Cup podium during his 10-year career, he did finish second twice and third
once. During the 1978–79 season, he even led the Canadian squad in overall
results, finishing third in the World Cup downhill standings.

Murray was named director of skiing at Whistler Mountain upon his
retirement in 1982—a position that appeared more honorific than practical at
the time. But Murray had other plans for the job. He was convinced that ski
racing in Canada was getting too elitist—too narrow in scope—and needed to
develop a broader base of participation. After all, he was a latecomer to the
sport himself (he didn't start to race seriously until he was 16). And he knew
from experience that racing could appeal to a much broader group of skiers.
Murray knew intuitively, too, that if he could entice more skiers into racing, he
could also foster greater interest on the part of potential sponsors.

With a partner, Don McQuaid, Murray formed the Masters' Group and
introduced the then-revolutionary concept of "adult racing" to Whistler and
completely changed the face of skiing in the region. Suddenly dentists,
lawyers, accountants and businessmen in Vancouver were buying stretchy
downhill suits and signing up for mid-week ski racing "camps" with Murray,
McQuaid and their all-star cast of coaches. When the world's best came to
Whistler to race, these new enthusiasts were out in force to watch and learn.

The mid 1980s was a time of tremendous growth at Whistler. And Murray,
and his wife, Stephanie Sloan, a former winner of the World Freestyle Ski
Championships, rode the wave like everyone else in town. Murray's adult racing programs flourished, bringing new sponsors flocking to the sport (just as
he had predicted). He became more involved—and more comfortable—as a

Before there was Boyd, there was Murray.

Whistler spokesman and was touted by some as a potential mayoral candidate
for the resort-municipality. It looked at the time as if there were little he couldn't
accomplish. But all of that changed when he was diagnosed with cancer.

Although he'd spent much of his last 20 years on the public stage, Murray
was an intensely private man, and chose to fight his final battles far from pry-
ing eyes. He was in and out of hospitals for months. Prodded, poked and operated on. Yet through it all, Murray bore his burden with grace and dignity. He
even managed a few windsurfing trips between hospital stays. When he
passed away on October 23, 1990, he was only 36 years old. His daughter, Julia,
was still in diapers. Whistler is a sadder place without him.

Boyd at play in his backyard. Unlike many of his European counterparts, Boyd was a skier first and a racer second.

it out of his mind. Two, three more powerful pushes with his ski poles. "Speed. Fast," he thinks. "Gotta get moving." And drops into his tuck, his elbows down below his knees, his hands curled up in front of his face. The hill drops away quickly—it only takes a few seconds for him to pass the 100-kilometers-per-hour mark. No time to enjoy the speed. No time for fear either. Just con-cen-trate. On your skis. On your body...

He reads the first bump perfectly. His skis barely lift up off the snow. Then the second. He rises up slightly for a moment, then drives his arms forward as he hits the crest. BLAM—he's in the air, compact and comfortable. He lands easily and screams through the compression on the edge of control. The roar of the crowd grows louder. He tries to ignore the storm of noise around him.

His skis are sliding well. He knows he's fast. "Stay focused," he croons to himself as he flies across the flats. "Work that ski." Now comes the hard part. A big round-house curve almost slam-dunks him into the ground. Then bang! A stomach-dropping flight down the Weasel. His skis slap down hard on landing, and he loses his bal-ance for just a moment. But he recovers quickly.

Boyd is concerned now. He knows the course is faster than it was during the training runs. But by how much?

On the next blind right-hander—where skiers lose sight of their line into the crucial Fallaway drop ahead—he realizes he hasn't made a big enough change of direction. "You're going way too straight," his brain screams at him.

He only has two options. Either he takes a chance and runs straight at the gate—a near-impossible line to maintain through the difficult sidehill curve—or he plays it safe, throws his skis sideways and regains his line. But "safe" has never been big in Boyd's lexicon. He decides to go for broke.

In a sport where a few inches often determine the difference between first and second, Boyd's move on the Fallaway turn is near suicidal. He passes the gate nearly two feet inside his predecessor's tracks and finishes his own turn way lower than anyone else, running a dan-gerous line inches away from the safety net at the bottom of the pitch. One wrong move here and he's gone. But he pulls it off.

The crowd is stunned into silence for a moment. No one expected this outrageous move. Then it erupts in an explosion of cheers. But Boyd is long gone. The lower half of the course beckons...

Boyd's skis accelerate quickly down the pitch below the Fallaway. He knows he's lost a bit of time, but he still

Above: A mountain trail at Whistler. When the snow melts and the days get longer, Whistler is transformed into a summer adventure paradise. Opposite: A man and his bike. A talented multi-disciplined ath-lete, Boyd is as much at home on two wheels as he is on two skis.

feels confident. "Got to make every turn count now." The second half of the course is a downhiller's nightmare—a maze of bumps and high-speed turns that can suck the energy out of fast-tiring muscles long before the skier reaches the finish line. One lapse of concentration—one backseat turn—and the race is over. But this is Boyd's strong suit. He knows he gets stronger as the race gets longer.

Boyd nails the next big right-hander perfectly and comes hurtling around Coaches' Corner like a man possessed. No one today has come through that turn with so much speed. The crowd roars its approval. "THE MID-POINT INTERVAL TIMES SHOW ROB BOYD IS NOW IN SECOND PLACE," screams the announcer. "LET'S BRING HIM ON HOME FOLKS. LET'S SHOW HOW WHISTLER SUPPORTS ITS OWN." The people massed in the finish area start to chant. Their voices grow louder and louder. GO-ROB-GO! GO-ROB-GO! GO-ROB-GO!

Boyd's parents—Sandy and Molly—stand with the others in the VIP enclosure at the bottom of the hill, barely able to suppress their excitement. It's their son, after all. And Whistler is their home, too. They know only too well what a victory would mean to Rob today. They also know what's at stake. But it's going to be close. Much too close to call it now.

Two very long minutes have elapsed since Boyd poled out of the starting gate. His legs are screaming in agony now, his lungs are tearing for more air. But he can't think of his pain—can't let his concentration lag. He grits his teeth and focuses on the problem ahead. One more jump. One last effort. He lunges forward and just clears the crest. His skis hit the snow hard. His legs feel like old rubber. He can barely hold on now. "Get lower, lower," he screams at himself. "PUSH IT TO THE END!"

And then it's over. He throws his skis sideways in the finish area and looks over his shoulder at the giant screen behind him. He knows he's had a good run. But was it good enough?

"THE NEW LEADER, LADIES AND GENTLE-MEN," cries the announcer, then pauses. "ROB BOYD OF CANADA, WITH A TIME OF TWO MINUTES 10 SECONDS and THREE THOUSANDTHS." Boyd has barely come to a stop when he's mobbed. Fans, friends, reporters, coaches, officials: everyone wants to be the first to congratulate him. Bulbs flash. Microphones appear from everywhere. The Whistler party to end all Whistler parties has just begun.

"It was an amazing time," says Boyd of his Whistler victory. We're standing high above the valley, getting ready to drop into one of our favorite runs on Whistler Mountain. His hair is shorter today than it was in 1989, and if you look closely you can find a few gray locks sprouting out here and there on his head. His face has more lines on it, too. And his body a few more scars. But that big-chin profile of his is still very much the same. "It was like I was floating on air for days afterward," he recalls. Laughs. "I don't remember much of what happened immediately after the race. It was all pretty much of a blur."

He smiles: "It took me a while to come off that particular high. I mean—I think most athletes dream of doing well in front of their home crowd. I was no different. To win in my backyard against the best in the world—it was truly a dream come true for me."

Boyd grew up in Vernon, B.C., a cozy little town in the interior of the province. His dad, Sandy, owned a small local ski hill—Tillicum Valley—and the family had the run of the place. "I remember," says Rob, "setting my own race course on the hill. I would zoom down that thing all day long." He laughs. "And no one could give me any guff, 'cuz my dad owned the place."

I first met Boyd in 1981. I was on my way to the Canadian Alpine Championships with a group of Vancouver athletes when I got a call from a coaching colleague based in Vernon. It turns out he had a young prospect that he wanted to send to the event, but there was nobody to take care of him there. Would I be able to take him under my wing for the next week?

Rob Boyd was barely 15 years old at the time. A tall, gangly kid with a mop of reddish blonde hair and an unpretentious demeanor, Boyd barely said a word the whole trip. He just let his skis do the talking for him. "At the time," he remembers, "I was still racing motorbikes. And doing pretty well at it. Skiing was definitely my second love."

But things were about to take a major turn in the life of the young athlete. Like so many other small ski resorts at the time, Tillicum Valley was struggling. And Rob's dad was looking around B.C. for new opportunities. When Whistler Mountain offered him the position of operations manager in 1982, Sandy decided to move his family west. "It was pretty intimidating at first," admits Rob of his new big-mountain home. "I'd never skied on anything this size before." But it took him little time to adapt. "I remember going on long motorbike trips with my dad. We'd explore every valley, every logging

1	BOYD, R.	CAN	2 10 03	17
2	MAHRER, D.	SUI	2 10 20	18
3	ZURBRIGGEN, P.	SUI	2 10 34	19
4	HOEFLEHNER, H.	AUT	2 10 71	20
5	HEINZER, F.	SUI	2 10 74	21
6	MUELLER, P.	SUI	2 10 78	22
7	PICCARD, F.	FRA	2 10 88	23
8	SKAARDAL, A.	NOR	2 10 91	24
9	WIRNSBERGER, P.	AUT	2 11 02	25
10	RUNGGALDIER, P.	ITA	2 11 05	26
	THORSEN, J. E.	NOR	2 11 24	27
	GIRARDELLI, M.	LUX	2 11 30	28
	ORTLIEB, P.	AUT	2 11 31	29
	BESSE, W.	SUI	2 11 34	30
	ZEHENTNER, H.	BRD	2 11 57	31
	ALPIGER, K.	SUI	2 11 63	

Boyd's win at Whistler was well-earned. To get to the top step of the podium, he had to beat four Olympic gold medalists.

road, every dirt track we could find. That was pretty cool."

That same year, Boyd was named to the B.C. Ski Team, an elite program for up-and-coming junior racers. But he still had a long way to go. "I was certainly not the star of the team," says Boyd with a chuckle. "I was just one of the pack."

And the pack was on the move. With the Olympics scheduled for Calgary in 1988, there was a fair bit of money kicking around in the early '80s for athlete development in Canada. And Boyd and his cohorts were identified early as worthy recipients. "The Crazy Canuck era was slowly coming to an end," he explains, "and the national team was desperate to develop a new cadre of athletes. So they spent a lot of money and effort on the junior program."

It seemed to work. The 1986 World Cup season had barely begun when Boyd had his first big breakthrough in Europe. His victory in Val Gardena, Italy, stunned everyone—including the Canadian Team coaches. "Here we were grooming these guys for the '92 Olympics," says Glen Wurtele, the mastermind behind the new Canadian downhill surge. "When we suddenly realized that they could be contenders in Calgary."

The next year, with only a few months remaining before the Olympics, Boyd repeated his feat in Italy. Only this time, his buddy Brian Stemmle was just a couple of steps down in third place. "Those were definitely exciting times," says Boyd. "But the pressure on us to do well in Calgary was almost overwhelming. Although our coaches did their best to shield us from the press, we knew what was expected of us."

The Olympic downhill was a bust for the Canadian men. And though Boyd continued to ski well (he finished the season among the top five overall in the World Cup downhill standings), the fortunes of the Canadians were definitely on a downswing. By the time of the 1989 World Cup downhill at Whistler, the team was in tatters. Boyd was the only one who could bring them back from the brink.

"For sure, my victory at Whistler was a big deal for the Canadian Team," he says. "But the problems ran too deep at the time for one good result to really change things around."

There would be more World Cup downhills at Whistler after 1989. In fact, in the early 1990s, there was a three-year streak—'93-'94-'95—where everything fell into place and the races were held without a hitch. But the Canadian Team continued to struggle. And the glory years of the Crazy Canucks and their high-spirited successors, Boyd, Stemmle et al., began to slowly fade from memory. Supporters—and sponsors—became more and more difficult to find.

Whistler organizers, however, were still keen on holding the event. They knew that the downhill was an important trump card in the promotion of Whistler on the international front. And they well understood the positive energy that it created among the residents of the valley. It was imperative, said members of the community-based W5 race organization, that the tradition be upheld.

But the Byzantine politics of the FIS, and the aggressive lobbying of the European resorts for prime-time exposure, forced their hand. By 1996, they had no alternative but to schedule their downhill race in early December—a dangerous decision given the resort's notoriously fickle weather at that time of the year.

"It seems to me," says Boyd, who has lived at Whistler since 1981, "that the decision was based more on emotions than on good sense." He laughs. "After all, anybody who has lived here for any amount of time knows that the best powder skiing often happens during those first weeks of December."

Three years in a row they tried to hold the race in December. Three years in a row they were shut down by bad weather. The Europeans mocked them. FIS officials said: "We told you so."

And the Canadians continued to slide down the pole of world rankings. "It was really tough on all of us," admits Boyd. "We badly needed early-season results in those years. And we all knew we could do it on the Whistler course. But we never got the chance."

Boyd retired in the spring of 1997. For nearly 15 years, he had carried the weight of expectations for the Canadian speed team. Three World Cup victories, many top-three finishes, and an easy-going leadership style had done much to prop up the ailing squad's fortunes. But his body was beginning to show signs of fatigue. And he wasn't getting any faster.

When Sidney Dawes and his Canadian Olympic Association (COA) cohorts flew up into Garibaldi Park in 1960 to inspect a prospective site for a future ski area on then-unknown London Mountain, few riding in the helicopter that day knew much about their destination. They were all searching for a site they could promote as the Canadian bid to host the 1968 Winter Olympic Games. And they really didn't care where that site was—as long as it was suitable.

But Franz Wilhelmsen—who was also on that trip—did care. He already had his eye on London Mountain. He also understood what a powerful tool the Olympic Games could be to his project. When it came time to build his resort, he wisely wrapped his new development project in the five-ringed flag of the Olympic movement.

And he remained true to that spirit. Whistler Mountain, at least in the early years, was all about ski racing. When Nancy Greene and the Canadian team stayed home from Europe in 1967 in order to race in the first Du Maurier International event at Whistler, the Vancouver skiing community came out en masse to support them. And they weren't disappointed. It was a great event. Outstanding, by all accounts. And it set the stage for many to come.

To his credit, Wilhelmsen seemed to be genuinely fond of ski racing. It appealed to his cosmopolitan ideals. All these exotic racers from the heartland of skiing. Austrian. Swiss. French. Italian. It brought an air of sophistication to the resort that Whistler badly needed in its early years. And Franz knew that. I remember watching him hold court in the finish area during Whistler's first World Cup event in 1975. He

looked so excited to be there. So happy. He reminded me of nothing so much as a proud father at his daughter's coming-out ceremony.

Over the next 25 years, Whistler Mountain would host nearly a dozen more World Cup events. Some were hugely successful. Some fell prey to bad weather or bad scheduling. Or just plain bad decision-making. In 1982, for example, the organizers decided to send the racers tortoising down the north side of the mountain in a poorly-conceived bid to promote the newly completed village. Even though Canadians finished second, third and fifth in that race, everyone agreed the old course was way more fun. By 1984, the racers were back on the Dave Murray course, scaring themselves silly again on the Sewer and Coaches' Corner and Fortnoy's. Although Whistler hasn't hosted a successful World Cup downhill event since the mid 1990s, many of its residents are still bullish about the sport. Enthusiasts around the valley would love nothing more than to see the top speedsters in the world return here to test their mettle on Whistler Mountain's slopes.

"It's still one of the most fun downhills in the world to race," asserts Rob Boyd. "And it deserves to be reinserted into the World Cup lineup. I just hope it comes back."

Whistler Mountain's first race.

Sunset over Rainbow Mountain.

"It's always tough to leave behind what you love," explains Boyd. "And I really struggled with my decision. But I also figured I had a lot of years left ahead of me to pursue new challenges. And I was keen to broaden my horizons."

That fall, Boyd was invited to captain the newly created Whistler Freeride Team. A squad of local skiing and snowboarding superstars, the Freeride Team was all about promoting mountain sports in the Whistler area. And Boyd took to the job with the same amount of positive energy he's always brought to new projects. "I loved World Cup racing," he says. "But I'd forgotten how much I loved free skiing as well."

"That's the great thing about living in Whistler," he explains. "For me, this place is all about mountain play. Sure it's home and all. But in my mind, Whistler isn't about the village and the amenities and the nightlife. It's about being in the mountains."

Pick an extreme sport—any extreme sport—and chances are good that Boyd is proficient at it. From skiing to snowboarding, mountain biking to moto-cross, windsurfing, wakeboarding or just plain mountain running—Boyd can play with the best. And often does. "Cutting new bike trails, hiking up mountains, finding new ski lines—that's what living at Whistler is all about for me. That's what keeps me here year after year."

Today, the man who shares his birthday with Whistler Mountain—February 15, 1966—is a thriving entrepreneur with interests in a local graphic arts studio, Toad Hall, and a hotel property on the east side of the Coast Range. He's also considering getting involved in ski racing again. But this time as a coach. "I've learned so much over the years—particularly about the need for balance between racing and free skiing—that I'd like to put some of these lessons to work."

The sun is much lower now than it was when we first started talking. The shadows are getting long, too. And though both of us enjoy these rare moments of solitude on "our" mountain, we both realize it's time to get off the peak. If we stay here much longer, we'll be skiing down in the dark. "Waddya say we start heading back down to the valley," suggests Boyd.

I'm all for it. But before I can even get up and click into my bindings, Boyd has jumped onto his skis and is already poling down the hill. "Race you to the bottom," he says. And then he's gone.

Above: Checking out the waves at Hookipa in the '90s. When it comes to trying new adventure sports, Boyd is no snob. Opposite: Mark "Toaster" Torley shoots the curl on Blackcomb Mountain.

CHAPTER 9
CHRISTIAN BEGIN

"It really bugs me when people whine about Whistler," says Christian Begin. A wild-haired hobbit of a guy whose

physical strength is camouflaged by his small frame—"I'm really a big man in a small container," he says with

a grin—Begin is a one-person verbal-assault squad.

"Don't get me wrong," he's quick to add. "I'm sad, too, that this valley is getting so urbanized. For sure, it's

lost a bit of its original charm But it's not like it's the end of the world. You just have to learn how to adapt your

life around it." His face slides into that slightly demented smile of his. "After all," he says, "it may be a cliché,

but you can't stop progress."

Suddenly he turns his attention to the meal in front of him. He shovels down a couple of forkfuls of potatoes and sops up some egg yolk with a hunk of bread. He wipes his mouth with the back of his hand. Sighs. And then takes a long draught of coffee. "Where was I?" he asks.

Christian Begin is not normal. Nor does he aspire to normality. An acclaimed filmmaker with an electric passion for life, the 39-year-old French Canadian is considered among the best high-energy-sports shooters in the world. He's also the guy who introduced the world to high-performance freeride mountain biking—and the B.C. hardcores who pioneered it—with his ground-breaking *Kranked* film trilogy.

"Yeah, I guess that's what I'm best-known for now," he says. "But to tell you the truth,"—and here he stares intently at me to make sure I get it—"I'd rather be known as a good storyteller. I want to make films that people will remember."

He stops for a microsecond. His eyes crinkle up tight. He giggles, and the hobbit connection is made even more apparent.

"You know what I mean? I'm not into making the film version of Big Macs. You know, I could make a lot more money just cranking out the same old stuff. But

that doesn't really make me happy. I want to do stuff that nobody else is doing."

We're sharing a booth at the Southside Deli, having a late breakfast. A longtime hangout for Creekside denizens, the deli is home to an assortment of colorful Whistlerites who live or work at this end of the valley. Admittedly, the deli's not much to look at. Nor is it particularly inviting to strangers. In fact, it's probably one of the more slovenly looking restaurants in Whistler. The room is dark, the furniture hasn't changed in 20 years, and many of the regulars look like they haven't slept in two or three days. But the food is good, and the owner, Cal, who presides behind the counter, is a great host.

I'm having the Eggs Oy Vey—a cholesterol explosion that adds great hunks of Montreal smoked brisket to the eggs Benedict theme. Christian is chowing down on the world-famous Belch. It's a sandwich with egg and ham and bacon and tomato and lettuce and cheese and all sorts of other great stuff. They say it's just the thing for hangovers.

His last bite now complete, Christian resumes his diatribe.

"C'mon, man," he says, his hands in the air to support his point of view. "Look at all the things you can still

Above: Begin at work. Combining a creative mind and an unflagging enthusiasm for adventure, Christian Begin has created a name for himself as one of the world's great adrenaline-sports filmmakers. Opposite: Begin at play. Much of his "feel" for film work is inspired by his own athletic experiences.

do around here. It's like a giant mountain playground, man. I can go ski touring in Garibaldi Park, mountain biking in Pemberton or windsurfing in Squamish. What's to complain about?"

That's why there are so many good photographers and filmmakers living at Whistler, adds Begin "We have athletes here who are pushing the level of sports performance every time they step outside their door. And that means that everyone else has to pick up their game, too."

Begin has always ridden on the farthest edge of the wave. Self-confident to the point of arrogance sometimes—and effusive in both French and English—Christian does his Quebecois roots proud. He's Jack Kerouac crossed with Ken Burns. Rocket Richard meets Spike Lee.

"I quit college when I was 18 and moved out to Banff to learn to speak English," he explains. "But I fell in love with the mountains instead." He sighs. "That's when I first realized Quebec would end up being too small a place for me."

Like most other Quebecois expatriates, however, his identity is still deeply embedded in the tendrils of his French-Canadian roots. "No matter where I choose to live, I'll always be partly Quebecois," he maintains. "That's who I am." He pauses. "But that doesn't mean I can't be proud to be a Canadian, too. I mean, given the beauty of the country, I'd be crazy to limit myself to just one part of it."

That's also why Begin loves the term "Franco-Columbian." "It's perfect man," he tells me. "It tells people where I came from. And it tells people where I am now. I have to admit that at first I didn't get it." He laughs. "But now, I use it all the time."

While it's not yet common currency in the province, Franco-Columbian refers to the fast-growing tribe of young Francophone men and women who now make their home in British Columbia. People like International Free Skiers Association world champion Hugo Harrison or his high-flying buddies Pierre-Yves Leblanc and Robin Courcelles, who all live in the Whistler area.

"There's no question," says Begin, who recently produced a film on Harrison for Rossignol skis, "we're different from our Anglo neighbors. Not better. Not worse. Just different. We're more passionate. We take more risks. We have more fun with life, I think."

From the very beginning, there was a Quebecois connection to Whistler Mountain. When flamboyant Prime Minister Pierre Elliot Trudeau married young Vancouver beauty Margo Sinclair in 1971, they spent part of their honeymoon in Alta Lake. And it was no great surprise to Whistler regulars. For Trudeau, in

those years, was a popular figure on the mountain's slopes. Pictures of him wedeling down Franz's run or heli-skiing with Jim McConkey often appeared in the newspapers back East. "For many people in eastern Canada," remembers McConkey, "this was their introduction to Whistler. Trudeau's association with the mountain, at a time when few skiers even knew about the place, made for a very glamorous connection."

While Trudeau was certainly the most famous French Canadian skier on the hill in those days, La Belle Province was already well represented at Whistler. Bob Dufour, Francois Lepine, and Rene Paquette were among the best skiers on the mountain in the early years. And no matter where the parties where, no matter who was celebrating, there always seemed to be a couple of Quebecois right in the thick of things.

"There's a connection with the Coast and B.C.," says Begin, "that French Canadians don't have with any other part of the country. Maybe it's because it's so far out on the edge of the world. Maybe it's because it such a cool place to be." He giggles again, like a kid in a candy store. "All I know is that it suits me."

Begin grew up in Quebec City and spent his youth skiing at nearby Mont-Sainte-Anne. "It was a great place to grow up," he says. "It's definitely one of the best pure-skiing resorts in eastern North America. And it nurtured a really strong mountain scene there."

But Begin was far too adventurous to be confined to the Quebec borders. On a ski trip to Switzerland in 1985, the 23-year-old found himself hanging out at Verbier with a bunch of filmmakers and photographers from Clambin Productions—John Falkner, Mark Shapiro, Ace Kvale and crew. And the young Quebecois was completely transported by their energy.

On his return to Quebec City, Begin got together with a bunch of skiing buddies at Mont-Sainte-Anne and decided to make his own movies. "I had just seen Greg Stump's new film, *The Blizzard of Aahhhs*. And I was blown away." He smiles. Slurps another dollop of coffee. "That was a huge turning point for me."

First came *Ski Radicale*, a science-fiction-cum-ski flick that was shot almost entirely at Quebec's spectacular Montmorency Falls. "It was extreme, man. And it was really funny." It came out in 1988, adds Begin, and it was completely inspired by *Blizzard*.

His second production changed his life.

"It was called *Transformer*," he says, "and it was seriously bent." He laughs. "You know, that was probably

For longtime Whistler locals, the Southside Deli is at once headquarters, shrine and clubhouse. And it offers a great breakfast too.

the first mountain-bike video ever made. And it was bad." His eyes crinkle again. "But we sure had fun making it."

Transformer ultimately would be the driving force behind Begin's move to the West Coast. "I was looking for sponsors. But everyone in the East kept laughing at me. I knew Stump was living at Whistler. And I figured he was my only hope. So I convinced my girlfriend to come west with me and see if we could enlist Stump's help in distributing my film."

The year was 1989. And Whistler was well on its way by then. As usual, housing was near impossible to find—especially for a struggling filmmaker. But Begin and his girlfriend lucked out. At least at first.

"The old caretaker's lodge at Rainbow was empty," he says. "So we moved right in."

Four months later they were back on the street.

"The municipality owned the cabin," he explains, "and they just decided one day that they didn't want anybody living there anymore. So they kicked us out."

With no other alternative in sight, the two young Quebecois decided to head back home.

Begin didn't stay long in Quebec. The mountains of B.C. were calling out too loudly. But he still couldn't afford to live at Whistler. So he did the next best thing and moved to Rossland, a legendary mountain town deep in the Kootenay Mountains of eastern B.C.

Nestled inside the caldera of a long-extinct volcano nearly 2,000 feet above the Columbia River (just before the great river crosses into the United States near the Washington-Idaho border), Rossland—and nearby Red Mountain—holds near-mythical status among Canadian skiers.

"On a good powder day," says Begin, his eyes aflame with excitement again, "Red Mountain is magical. For off-piste glade skiing, there is nowhere better in the world."

Begin spent the next four years in Rossland. In 1994, he started work on the film that would provide him with his first big breakthrough, *Locomotion*.

A sort of docu-adventure homage to the men who pushed the railroad across Canada's near-impenetrable Rogers Pass nearly 130 years ago, *Locomotion* was a pastiche of ghostly scenes of skiers, wild avalanche sequences and archival footage of the building of the CP railroad. It was like nothing anyone had seen before.

"You know," he bursts, "without that railroad, our country would have never gone from sea to sea." He takes a quick breath. "Besides, it's because of the opening of Rogers Pass that we can ski these beautiful B.C. mountains. No other reason. That's why I made that film. I wanted the new generation to understand what was up."

The gateway to some of the most exhilarating back-country terrain on the planet, Rogers Pass is now a favorite with self-propelled skiers and snowboarders from across North America. But back in 1994, when Begin made *Locomotion,* the area was little known to anyone outside western Canada.

"It's amazing to think of what they were able to accomplish there," says Begin of the 19th-century rail project that finally opened up the Interior of B.C. to the rest of the world. "Hundreds of men died—and thousands more were injured—just so they could push a rail line to the Pacific. At the time, it was one of the biggest engineering feats ever accomplished."

Never a man to take the easy route, Begin chose to film *Locomotion* in the most authentic way he could. "Most ski films are shot using helicopters and lifts and snowmobiles," he explains. "Well, I didn't want to go that route, man. I felt it would have been betraying the memory of the men who died working on the pass. Instead, we climbed for all our shots. Every frame in that film was earned honestly. I mean—it was self-propelled guerilla filmmaking at its best." He laughs like a crazy man. "And at its most dismal, too."

Not surprisingly, a number of Whistler skiers also appeared in the film. "There was Pete Smart and Greg Dobin and Johnny Chilton," remembers Begin. "And they were all top-notch guys. As it turns out, *Locomotion* was my introduction to the local big-mountain crew. You know—guys like Trevor Petersen and Eric Pehota; Trevor's wife, Tanya; Jia Congdon, Swede Mattsson, Bruce Rowles..."

At the time, Whistler was a hotbed of adventure filmmaking. "It was almost overwhelming," admits

OF MEN AND BIKES AND IMPASSABLE FORESTS

Rob Boyd had this "little" trip in mind, and he wanted me to come along. "I figure we could circumnavigate the Cloudburst massif on our [mountain] bikes," he said. "Should be a fun adventure."

I should have known better.

Cloudburst is the southern gateway to the Whistler Valley, a beautiful-looking mountain with steep, snow-choked alpine bowls and a relatively low timberline. From an altitude of 6,136 feet, it drops almost all the way to sea level. The Cheakamus River runs on one side, the Squamish on the other.

Rob's plan was simple. All we had to do, he said, was ride and climb up the northwest flank of Cloudburst, drop down the other side to the upper Squamish, follow it all the way to its confluence with the Cheakamus, then climb back up to Whistler via the old Cheakamus Canyon trail. It was a full day's travel, but one that seemed well within our means. "Five, six hours' effort, max," Boyd said with a straight face.

First, we hammered our way over familiar trails to the head of the logging road that leads to the base of Cloudburst. Although the logging road was steep, we maintained a pretty good pace all the way to the head of the pass. It was still early in the morning, and the view was stupendous. Across the valley, Black Tusk thrust mightily into the sky. Directly south, Brohm Ridge and Diamondhead presented an alpine skyline almost too perfect to behold. "Not a bad view," said Boyd with a smile. "At this pace we'll be back in Whistler in no time."

But there was just one hitch: Although both the north side and the west side of Cloudburst had been logged, the mountain pass connecting the two clear-cut areas had not. And there were no trails connecting the two logging slashes.

"It'll only be a half-mile slog or so," said Boyd reassuringly as he shouldered his bike and disappeared into the jungle-like underbrush. "Don't worry."

The half-hour slog stretched into a two-and-a-half-hour enduro hike. With my bike on my back, I felt like a convict on a chain gang. Muck up to our ankles, mosquitoes and black flies and deer flies and no-see-ums buzzing around our heads—the aptly named devil's club tearing at our clothes—we bobbed and weaved blindly through the underbrush in search of deliverance.

Just as I was ready to give up and turn back, we reached the edge of the clear-cut. Neither one of us had ever been so happy to see the devastating scars of man's logging activities before. Just below us was the twisting ribbon of logging road that would soon carry us down to the Squamish River. We were saved.

Maybe not. First we had to cross the clear-cut—which turned out to be an even nastier enterprise than getting through the bush. Balancing your way along a massive cedar log high above the ground with a bike on your back tests agility skills like few other activities. Things had to get better soon.

Which they did. The view from the west flank of Cloudburst was spectacular. To the north and west stretched the massive glaciated peaks of the Tantalus range. High over our heads, a pair of bald eagles surfed the afternoon updrafts from the Squamish Valley. "Kind of beautiful place we live in," said Boyd. "Nice to have it all to ourselves, too."

For the next half hour on our bikes, we seemed to fly, dropping down the nearly 3,000 vertical feet that separated us from the upper Squamish like jet fighters on a mission. I was hard-pressed to keep Boyd's hunched-over form in sight. It was over much too soon.

Tunnel vision comes easily after 8-9 hours on a bike.

Not having a map, we weren't exactly sure how far upstream we'd hit the river. MILE 26, said the sign. Twenty-six miles to Squamish? "Just a little jaunt, eh," I taunted Rob. It was already well into the afternoon, and we were barely halfway home. We put our heads down and started spinning in earnest. Every now and then, a logging truck would scream by, covering us in a fine shower of gravel dust.

The road seemed endless, and the hot sun sizzled over our heads unmercifully. We were out of water, out of food and fast approaching our limits. By the time we reached the Cheakamus River, we were exhausted. The thought of the long climb back up to Whistler had us both nearly sobbing in despair.

There was nothing memorable about the rest of the trip. Despite the beauty of the century-old track that winds its way up the Cheakamus Canyon, or the mighty sunset that splashed pinks and oranges across the sky for our private viewing pleasure, we kept our heads down.

The highway was a long time coming. And the last miles home were slow to roll under our wheels. Finally, Whistler's Creekside base came into view. I checked my watch. Our "little" trip had taken more than nine hours. "I gotta eat something soon," croaked Boyd as we approached the first cluster of restaurants that signaled our arrival home.

"Me, too. Do you wanna go to your house first and have a shower?"

He shook his head. "I don't think I have the strength. Let's just stop here and get a big plate of pasta."

So that's what we did.

Begin switched from ski filming to bike filming mainly because he was tired of freezing his fingers.

Jia Condon defies gravity
on a local ice climb.

Begin, who edited most of *Locomotion* here. "There were so many good shooters. Greg Stump, Peter Chrzanowski, Beat Steiner, David Frazee, Jacques Roiseux—it was really inspiring."

As much as he loved his laid-back lifestyle in the Kootenays, Rossland was getting too small for Begin. He had no choice, he decided. He had to move back to Whistler—no matter how much it was going to cost him.

"I lucked out again," he says. "There was this old cabin—next to the train tracks down by Creekside—called The Trap. Built in 1929 or something. A real classic—round logs, sloping floor, the works. But it was cheap, so I decided to move in."

He hasn't moved since.

"I've always loved old houses," he says. "When I lived in Quebec, I lived only in old places." They have a special cachet, he explains, that you just don't get in a modern house. "It's more like Europe, more chalet-like than city home. And I like that."

As it turned out, 1995 was a watershed year for Begin. "Greg Stump had a contract with Specialized to produce a film on mountain biking that year," he explains. "And he remembered my stuff from *Transformer*. So he got hold of me and said: 'Christian, I

have to do this biking film, and I don't have time to do it. Do you think you could shoot some of it for me?'" Begin didn't need to be asked twice.

Again, he decided to shoot the footage his way. He'd heard rumors from some Whistler riders about this incredibly steep riding terrain near Kamloops in B.C.'s Interior. "So I asked Brett Tippie and Richie Schley about it," remembers Begin. "And they were really enthusiastic. They said the stuff was sick. Totally out there. So that's where we went to shoot."

The resulting film, *Pulp Traction*, created quite a buzz in the mountain-biking community. And while it was definitely a Stump film, much of the ruckus focused on the extreme segments shot by Begin.

"Not everyone was ready for it," he admits. "For starters, I think the people at Specialized were shocked by what we showed them. After all, nobody in the U.S. had ever seen anything like this before."

And nobody was quite ready for the reckless abandon of the B.C. riders.

"Remember—at that time, there was no rear suspension to the bikes and virtually no protection," says Begin. "The athletes were taking it where no one had taken it before."

For adrenaline junkies, Whistler is paradise. Whether it's extreme rafting (opposite) or single-track riding (below), the region offers up a cornucopia of sporting alternatives.

John Chilton negotiates the
frozen shark's teeth of
Blackcomb Peak.

Springtime has always been big at Whistler. After all, what's not to like about longer days and warmer sunshine?

"In the early years [at Whistler Mountain]," recalls Hugh Smythe, "we did some of our biggest numbers during the May long weekend. I can remember being pelted with snowballs by irate customers one day because the liftlines were so long."

While other ski areas are shutting down their lifts and running inventory on their cafeteria supplies, Whistler is girding itself for a second snow season that defies the senses. Increasingly—for North American enthusiasts at least—Whistler is the place to be from late March until early June.

"If you're serious about being part of what's happening, it's almost mandatory to pass through Whistler sometime during that period," says Christian Begin. "Everyone comes here. No matter if you're a pro rider, photographer or a filmmaker." He laughs. "Besides—it's not like it's a bad thing. Spring skiing around here is sweet."

No question. Whistler is at its most appealing at this time of the year. Often brilliantly green in the valley, and still ghostly white in the alpine region, it offers up a cornucopia of cross-seasonal activities unmatched anywhere. It's the time of year where you can go for a bike ride on the valley trails in the morning, take the lifts up the mountain for a midday ski and come back down in time for a round of golf, a sail on the lake or a paddle down the river.

Maybe that's why Doug Perry's World Ski and Snowboard Festival (WSSF) has been such a hit in recent years. Officially launched in 1996, the 10-day WSSF is a hard-pumping tribute to Whistler in springtime: a potent brew of 21st-century snow-sport contests, leading-edge musical shows and cultural events. It's a kaleidoscope of memorable moments. A youthful celebration of sun and snow. Kids in shorts and T-shirts hanging out with their friends, listening to their favorite rock bands playing live in the village square. Others in floppy pants and baggy jackets standing on the side of the slope, watching the world's best New Schoolers doing their thing in the snow-cross course or the halfpipe. Breaking new ground with each leap. Pushing the boundaries with every turn. Its top-level photography contests and quirky filmmaking challenges hold court in the convention center. There are ski-and-board tests, fashion shows and, above all, lots of riding.

And it couldn't happen anywhere else but at Whistler.

"I think springtime is an important part of the sport," says Perry. "Whether you're a snowboarder or a skier, it really doesn't matter. Everyone loves spring riding. And that was a prime motivator for me in putting together the event."

Left and above: The world's best bring their best to Whistler in the spring, and the crowds come out to cheer them on.

Meanwhile, *Locomotion* was garnering its own attention.

"It all happened so fast," he says. "I won Best New Filmmaker at the Crested Butte Adventure Film Festival, and *Locomotion* made the world tour of the Banff Film Festival. It was pretty exciting." And it opened all sorts of doors for the young filmmaker.

His next ski-film project—*No Man's Land*—went where no filmmaker had ever gone before. "I always had this idea that a high-performance ski/snowboarding film strictly on women would go over really well," he explains. "I love women. I love extreme women even more. And I figured there were others out there like me." He sighs, shakes his head. "It took me two years to make that film. And it nearly broke me. But I'm very proud of the final product."

Like *Locomotion*, his latest film also featured local Whistler riders. Hard-charging women like Wendy Brookbank, Victoria Jealouse and Lee Anne Patterson. And it showed them doing what they do best: skiing and riding as hard as the men. But it did it without being condescending—or smarmy. And people in the ski business started to pay even more attention to Begin's work. "That's when I connected with the guys at *Powder* and *Bike* magazines," he says. "They were the first ones in the States to really understand what I was trying to do in those years."

It was just the connection he needed.

When his new partner, Bjorn Enga ("after *No Man's Land*," says Begin, "I decided never to do another film by myself")—told him *Bike* was looking for ideas for a new TV show, Begin says he knew exactly what he wanted to do. "I sent Bjorn back to the folks at *Bike* magazine to pitch them on a B.C.-only segment. And I added a real sweetener to the deal. As long as they paid our production costs, they could use all our material for free." The only caveat? "All the footage would revert back to us after they used it. And we could make our own film with it."

Freeriding in B.C., which appeared on the show in August 1996, was the ultimate madman's mountain-bike travelogue. And it celebrated the special nature of B.C.'s riding community like nothing that had been produced before. "We shot all over the province—Whistler, the North Shore of Vancouver, Kamloops, the Kootenays—we didn't miss a location."

Until that point in the United States, mountain biking had been depicted as a fairly staid activity. Fire-road descents in northern California and long alpine rides in the Four Corners area of southwestern Colorado was about as wild as it got back then.

Above: Carving a turn in the skate park. Whether in summer or in winter, some of the world's top athletes now make their home at Whistler.
Opposite: Big air for bikers. The freeride ethos was quick to take root in the Whistler biking community.

"Nobody had a clue what was up here," says Begin.

But they soon found out. For the wild, mountainous terrain of southern B.C. had spawned a two-wheeled backcountry culture that was as bold as it was talented. Led by a posse of Whistler riders, Begin's crew attacked the unforgiving terrain with serious abandon. Sickeningly steep descents through old-growth forests of spruce and fir and cedar; log rides over yawning chasms where one bad move spelled instant disaster; harrowing crashes on 50-degree slopes, brain-bending leaps over scary gaps—it was all there. All part of the new cycling order called *Freeriding in B.C.*

Armed with this new footage, Begin and Enga decided to mount a frontal attack on the bike industry. "We went to the Anaheim bike show in California [the biggest of its kind in the world] with a teaser from *Freeriding in B.C.,*" remembers Begin. "I had this little portable TV under my arm, and we'd show our teaser to whoever would watch. And you know what?" Another bout of laughter. "We were the hit of the show. Suddenly all these B.C. riders—Tippie, Schley, Chris Lawrence, Dave Sutherland and Wade Simmons—were signing major endorsement contracts."

And Begin and Enga had their first big bike movie

deal. *Kranked* came out in the spring of 1998, And it changed the face of bike movie-making forever.

"That film was the first real coming-out party for B.C. freeriding," says its director. "Suddenly people around the world were seeing just how progressive the riders from Whistler and Vancouver and Kamloops and Rossland really were." He laughs. "They also noticed how sick the riding is on the coast of B.C. It made a lot of people want to come up here and ride."

A review of the film in *Bike* magazine illustrates just how much the industry was rocked by what Begin had shot: "With unbelievable descents, mind-blowing drops and never-seen-before maneuvers, *Kranked* is on the cutting edge of mountain-bike filmmaking...This flick will do for mountain biking what *Blizzard of Aahhhs* did for skiing."

Begin was bowled over by all the attention. Suddenly he was being hailed as a filmmaking visionary, even being mentioned in the same breath as his idol, Stump. It was all a little too much for the young filmmaker.

But Begin and Enga knew they had a winning formula. And they decided to milk it for all it was worth.

They produced two more *Kranked* films—the second in 1999 and the third in 2000—essentially revisiting the same themes that had been so well outlined in their first

Opposite: Redefining the limits of the possible. When Begin's first full-length mountain bike movie, *Kranked*, was released, its "go-for-it" philosophy took the North American riding community by storm.
Below: Begin briefs his riders. Passionate about his work, Begin never hesitates to push the boundaries of adventure filmmaking.

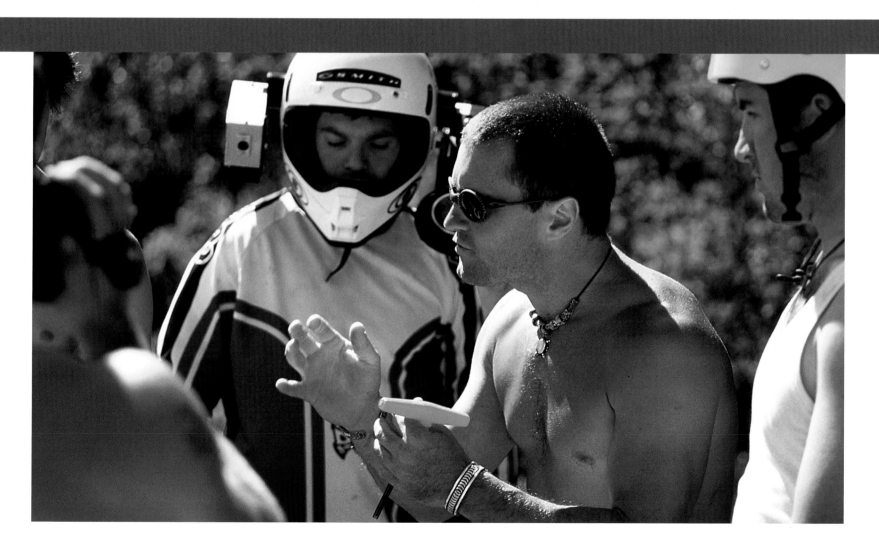

production. But Begin wasn't happy.

"I got burned out after doing essentially the same film three times in a row." He snorts. "You know—I could have done 10 *Kranks*. And then I would have probably had enough money to retire. But for me, that's too much like shooting pornography. It's fun to do for a while. But it's limited."

So Begin is branching out again. He's returned to his first love—skiing—and he is doing a lot more commercial work with sponsors and promoters. He's also embarked on a new venture with filmmaker Beat Steiner and mountain guide Peter "The Swede" Mattsson. "We've put together this proposal for a new heli-ski operation up the coast in Bella Coola. It's an amazing place. Probably some of the best skiing I've seen anywhere."

With the launch of this new wilderness-skiing operation, Begin and his partners face many of the same challenges that confronted Franz Wilhelmsen back in 1960 when he launched Garibaldi Lifts. "Too big, too isolated, too stormy," people say of the mountains around Bella Coola. "It will never work." And they have a point. A remote Indian village located halfway up the coast of B.C., Bella Coola, at first glance, does not appear to be an ideal location for a high-end tourist des-

tination. It's at least a two-day road trip by car from Vancouver. And in the winter, the roads are often impassable. Clients can also be flown in, of course. That is, if the notoriously nasty coastal weather cooperates. But Begin appears to be unmoved by the naysayers.

"We want to develop a ski/snowboarding resort for top-notch experts," he says. "People who appreciate what it means to get away from it all." He smiles. And a bit of an edge comes into his voice. "This is not for wimps, you know. This is for people with a real sense of adventure."

Breakfast is long over. We're on our fifth or sixth cup of coffee now, and Cal, the owner, is starting to give us the hairy eyeball. Two or three different waves of patrons have come and gone. He needs the table.

"So what are you doing now?" Begin wants to know. And then, before I can answer, throws in: "I'm going to Pemberton to check out this new bike trail. Big vert. Long ride. They say it's awesome. You want to come along?"

I nod. "Just give me time to grab my gear."

"Okay, okay. But we should go soon," he says. He's already fidgeting. Already thinking of his next adventure. "So I'll see you at my place in 15 minutes. Is that cool?" And with that, he gets up, throws his fleece jacket back on and, with a goodbye wave to Cal, slips out the door.

Above: Begin's newest venture is operating heli-skiing trips in the remote Coast Mountains of northern B.C.
Opposite: Between land and snow. With the growing popularity of adventure mountain biking, Whistler is becoming once again a much sought-after summer destination.

CHAPTER 10
BRITT JANYK

On the one side, she's heir to a Canadian ski racing tradition that stretches over half a century. From Lucille

Wheeler to Anne Heggtveit, from Nancy Greene-Raine to Kerrin Lee-Gartner, Canada's women skiers have always

had a powerful presence on the world stage. On the other side, she's heir to a local racing tradition that is just

as honorable (if not quite as long). From Dave Murray to Rob Boyd, John Smart to Ross Rebagliati, Whistler's

snowsport athletes have always done well in international competition.

Britt Janyk only hopes that she can do justice to both sides. At 22, the reigning Europa Cup champion is just

coming into her own. Yet she knows there's a long way to go. "I'm not the kind of athlete who has these huge

jumps in performances," she says. "I'm more the grinder type. I just keep moving along, progressing steadily." She smiles. And the little-girl dimples that appear suddenly on her cheeks take five years off her age. "But that's good enough for me. As long as I improve a little every season."

We are sitting in a VIP lounge at the Vancouver Airport. Britt is on her way to another training camp in Austria. With her water bottle and her computer, her sensible shoes and comfortable jacket, she looks more like a university student than a professional athlete. It's only the deep tan on her face and the sharp look in her eyes that hints of something more. But it's just a hint.

In an age when ski racers are seemingly becoming bigger and stronger every year—more like burly-thighed linebackers than nimble-footed acrobats—Britt Janyk is something of an anomaly. She's short, not more than a couple of inches over five feet tall, and not at all imposing in stature. Not petite exactly. Nor dainty. Just contained. She looks like the girl next door. Fun to hang with. A great friend. Not a threat.

But don't underestimate her abilities. For while she may not display the plumage of a conventional ski-racing superstar, she may just get there anyway. A triple

gold medalist at the 2002 Canadian Championships—she won the giant slalom, the super G and the combined event—Britt is one of the most exciting young prospects on the national team today. And it's precisely because her progress has been so steady that she's hot.

Without fanfare, without histrionics of any kind, Britt has quietly worked her way up the international ranking ladder. Nothing fancy. Nothing out of the ordinary. Just really consistent results. Today, the top rung is well within her reach.

"She's certainly somebody worth watching over the next few years," agrees Rob Boyd. "I really like how she stands on her skis. She's very natural. Very relaxed. Yet she's deceptively powerful."

She's also a highly versatile athlete.

"Soccer was really big for me when I was young," she says. "So was gymnastics. I'm sure both those sports have helped me develop the speed and agility I need for ski racing."

She laughs. "I was pretty darn good at gymnastics, too. But I had to drop it when they told me I'd have to train weekends. 'There's no way,' said my mum to the gymnastics coach. 'We're skiers. On weekends we're at the mountain.'"

Above: On the hunt. She's not that big. And she doesn't come across as particularly aggressive. But her drive and determination have carried Britt Janyk to the top strata of women's ski racing.
Opposite: With dad on the mountain. Although she tried her hand at a variety of sports as a kid, ski racing was always number one for Britt.

Youth culture has always played a big part in the Whistler story.

ROSS REBAGLIATI: OLYMPIC GOLD

His name is pronounced "RA-blee-AH-tee." And he's the owner of the first snowboarding gold medal ever awarded in the history of the Olympic Winter Games. He also owns his own home at Whistler ("the house that snowboarding bought," he says proudly) and drives a big fancy pickup truck perma-stuffed with snowboards and water skis and surfboards and windsurfers and mountain bikes.

Yet the 1998 Olympic hero they call Reebag insists he's still just one of the guys. "I've been a competitor all my life," says the 31-year-old. "And I've learned a lot. For sure, it's easy to get caught up in the whole circus and get carried away with your own self-importance." He smiles, like a 10-year-old grommet caught with too many candies in his hands. "Luckily I have good friends. The same ones I've been hanging with since I was in grade school. They know me like nobody else does. And they don't let me get away with squat."

Ross doesn't race much anymore. He doesn't have to. His gold-medal performance in Nagano, Japan, combined with all the media attention he received from getting disqualified for traces of marijuana found in his urine sample—then immediately getting reinstated on a technicality—gave him the 15 minutes of fame he needed to set himself up as an independent businessman.

For the record, he insists he did not smoke marijuana prior to his competition. He maintains he inadvertently inhaled second-hand smoke at a wake for a close friend just before leaving Whistler for the Games. Also for the record:

The fact that Ross got busted for pot at the Olympics only served to cement Whistler's reputation with the youth market as a very cool place to visit.

Yet there is an irony here. For the athlete who was both lionized and vilified by pro- and anti-pot advocates, Ross had spent much of his career cultivating an image that was radically different from the mainstream, droopy-pants gangsta boardhead look. Think preppy. Think Dartmouth Ski Team in the '50s. Think straight.

"I got tired really quickly of the poseur outlaw rider style," he told me back in 1996. "I wanted to come across as a professional. A guy who meant business." In the late '80s, he spent the better part of a season competing wearing a sweatshirt with "Be a Boardhead, Not a Drughead" on its back. "It made people realize that boarders come in all shapes and sizes. All kinds of backgrounds, too."

There is no doubt Reebag has made his mark in the world of professional sports. And there's no doubt he's learned a lot from his journey to the top rankings. "My role now," he says, "is to be as humble as possible. People who know me don't care about my snowboarding results or my Olympic gold. That was just my job. That's what I did for a living. I didn't do it for the image thing." Another smile. Another hint of the madman hiding behind the understated delivery. "I did it 'cause I love to go fast."

Above: From hero to zero and back to hero, all because of a little secondhand smoke.
Left: Thousands of fans jammed the streets of Whistler to welcome their newest hero home.

Britt's story is fascinating. She comes from one of the true ski-pioneering families in B.C. Her Hungarian grandfather, Peter Vajda, built North America's first two-seater chairlift in 1949 on Vancouver's Grouse Mountain. Her mother, Andree—"one of the most outgoing, energetic women I know," says Whistler pro ski patroller Cathy Jewett—was a hard-charging member of the Canadian Alpine Ski Team in the late '60s. Although Britt lived the first 14 years of her life in West Vancouver, her winters were spent mostly at Whistler.

"My earliest memories," she says, "are of skiing in the front yard of our Whistler cabin. Practicing how to put on and take off my gear so that my mum and dad would finally allow me to ski the big mountain. And I really cherish those memories. For me, skiing has always been a fun thing. Never a chore."

Skiing was also very much a social event for the Janyk family. "Skiing was our life during the winter season," she adds. "We didn't miss a weekend from December until April." She stops. Laughs again. It's a great laugh, too—unforced and easy-going, infectious. "I remember these great gangs of kids and parents, all skiing together. Big kids, little kids—it was loads of fun."

Before there were international tourists, before it became the number one mountain resort in North America, Whistler Mountain was essentially a weekend area for Vancouver skiers. One group, in particular, took advantage of the situation. Barely an hour's drive from the slopes of Whistler, the middle-class communities of North and West Vancouver teemed with young sports-minded families in the mid 1970s. Many of these families were introduced to skiing at Grouse or Mt. Seymour, located minutes away from their homes. But as the kids grew up, the small local hills just didn't cut it anymore.

Enter Whistler. While it meant a considerably longer drive, skiing at Whistler was just the thing these young families needed to keep their kids challenged—and entertained. Not to mention providing mum and dad with a little more fun, too. The Whistler Mountain Ski Club (WMSC) was founded in 1968, two years after the area opened. Dominated, in large part, by families from Vancouver's North Shore (at least in the early years), the WMSC was soon one of the most powerful clubs in the province. And one of the best at holding big-time races.

From the 1969 Canadian Skiing Championships to the 1995 World Cup races, from its legendary Backbowl downhills to its hugely popular Whistler Cup juvenile races, the WMSC has always set the standard in Canada

for well-run, well-financed competitions. The 2002 Canadian Championships was a perfect example of this, says Britt: "Our nationals were just as good—and just as well-organized—as any World Cup event I've attended in Europe."

That's why, she adds, she was so happy to perform well in Whisler. "To win three gold medals on my home mountain was very satisfying," she admits. "Particularly since you don't get that kind of opportunity too often in this sport. But for me, it was also a tribute to all the work that the Weasel Workers, the Whistler Club members, and Whistler/Blackcomb crew had put into our races. A

Britt with some of her newly-acquired hardware. Like Dave Murray and Rob Boyd before her, Britt is an easy-going, unassuming Whistler athlete who'd much rather hang with her friends than schmooze with the big wigs.

smooth-running event makes a huge difference to an athlete's performance. And the volunteers who work the Whistler races really know how to do that."

But the quality of its ski racing program is just one of Whistler's special attributes, says Janyk. Like so many other Whistler racers—Dave Murray and Rob Boyd come immediately to mind—Britt insists that she's a skier first and a racer second.

"Until I joined the race club at 11," she says, "the only gates I'd skied in on the public ski-machine course." Freeskiing was a blast when she was a kid. Besides, she says, exploring the slopes of Blackcomb was way too much fun to succumb to a regimented program too early. "We had this little gang—family and friends and stuff— and we'd bomb around together all day. Then we'd go sledding while the adults had their après-ski."

Britt's mountain posse included her younger brother, Michael, another up-and-coming member of the Canadian Team, and to a lesser extent, her sister, Stephanie, "who's more into the 'drama' side of things," she says. "And we skied everywhere. On the groomed, in the bumps, in the trees, over jumps. Whatever struck our fancy that day. We had our favorites, of course. But we did it all."

As a training ground for young skiers and riders, the multifaceted slopes of Whistler/Blackcomb are hard to beat. The runs are long. The snow is deep. And the terrain is inexhaustible. Especially for kids. "Whistlerites are famous around the world for their go-for-it attitude," says Rob Boyd. "They charge harder. Go faster. And take more risks than just about anybody out there. But that's just the Whistler style. It's the way the mountains around here taught us how to ski."

Britt is quick to agree. "Because I've been traveling a lot in recent years, I often get asked: 'What's your favorite resort to ski?'" She smiles. "There are some pretty amazing places in Europe, for sure, but for me, it just doesn't get much better than what we have right here."

She pauses again. "You know, there's something special about flying into the Vancouver airport and passing over the Coast Mountains and the Pacific Ocean. It's really magical for me. Really beautiful. It's at those moments that I feel really fortunate to be living here."

She laughs. "I'm a Coast Mountain girl through and through. I love the mountains and I love the ocean. There's nowhere else I could imagine living. When I eventually retire from this sport, I'm not planning on moving anywhere else."

While she wasn't in any hurry to start racing gates, something clicked when she eventually decided to get involved with the club.

"I couldn't get enough of it," she says. "Being part of the Whistler Club was a huge asset for me. I'm not sure I could have had the same success if I'd grown up in another program. During those early years, I was fortunate to have some really good coaches—and really good racers—to train with."

For the first few years, ski racing was just a fun extension of her weekend visits to Whistler. Then she started to do well. In no time, Britt found herself totally involved in the ski racing world. Traveling to Europe to compete at the World Juvenile Championships. Going to special training camps for promising juniors. Getting a lot of attention.

"It all happened pretty quickly," she says.

By the time Britt was 14—and her brother, Michael, 12—her parents were considering leaving West Vancouver for good.

"It got to the point," explains Britt, "where my mum and dad were driving up Highway 99 just about every day. The high schools in the city didn't cooperate very much with my travel demands. Everything was just so complicated."

So the family decided to move up to Whistler. And once the decision was taken, the Janyks never questioned it again. Britt entered Whistler High School at the beginning of grade 10. "And because the staff there understood better what ski racing was about," she says, "I was able to graduate on time with my peers and still maintain my competitive schedule."

But it wasn't all that easy. "I was really sad to leave West Vancouver. I had a lot of close friends there. It was really tough to realize I wouldn't be graduating with them. But at the same time, I knew the move made a lot of sense. If I was to become a successful ski racer, then it was the only smart thing to do."

The transition was surprisingly smooth. The Janyk kids already had a lot of ski racing friends at Whistler. The school administration was far more understanding about elite sports than its counterpart in the city. And the club was only too happy to have them in the program. Besides, the community was still small enough then that it could easily absorb young families. In no time, the Janyks were completely immersed in the daily life of their new mountain home.

And no one got more immersed in community life than did Britt's mother, Andree.

"My mum isn't really happy unless she's really busy," says Britt. Most people who know her mother would consider that a whopping understatement. Like Nancy Greene-Raine before her, and Myrtle Philip before that, Andree Janyk has become a very active member of the local school board. She's also a full-time ski instructor at Blackcomb in the winter and she launched, and now runs, the local kids' soccer league.

"She's a very impressive person," says Cathy Jewett, herself a bit of an energy bomb. "She just never seems to run out of steam."

"I owe an awful lot to my parents," adds Britt. "For their positive attitude. For their energy. For everything. Ski racing isn't a cheap sport. And they've both made huge sacrifices to get us where we are now. But they've never complained. They chose to make the move up here because they saw great opportunities for us. And I don't think they've ever regretted it. How could they? We've all learned so much from it."

Today, seven years after the move from West Vancouver, Britt says she can't imagine living anywhere else but Whistler.

"I've had such a great time here," she says. "The high school at Whistler was really tiny compared to

where I came from—less than 350 students from grade seven to 12. So the class sizes were small and you got a lot of attention from the teachers. In that way, it was way more like a private school than a public school."

Being a local racer also meant that she drew a lot more attention and support at Whistler than she would have in the city.

"When you're a local athlete," says Cathy Jewett, "you get a lot of local people rooting for you. And a lot of goodwill going your way. I don't know if it's the same for other communities, but Whistlerites do really get involved with their own."

No question about it, says Britt: "It's a big resort now. But there is a real community here, too. And a very supportive one. Local people are genuinely interested in what I do. And it's the same for every athlete who has grown up here. Maybe it's because the very nature of living at Whistler—the tourists, the glitz, the big-time money—can be really overwhelming at times. And this is a way for the community to compensate. Whatever. It's been great for me."

She stops talking for a moment. Reflects on the right words she wants to use. "You know—most people don't realize it, but Whistler still has a small-town feel when it

Above: **Britt sets up for a pass. Soccer has always been a big thing in the Janyk household.**
Opposite: **Rob Boyd rips it up in the alpine zone. Like Boyd and most other ski racing alumni from Whistler, Britt still believes in the power of freeskiing.**

There is a notorious section of Whistler's Dave Murray Downhill course, roughly a third of the way down the run, that's been the downfall of more than one international star. No wonder. Racers come skittering around a big, blind right-handed turn off the Toilet Bowl flats and get slammed down what racers call The Weasel—a 200-meter-long section of the course that is among the steepest in the world.

"There's nothing else quite like it," says Rob Boyd. "If you're not right on top of your skis when you hit the compression at the bottom of The Weasel, you're probably not going to get much farther down the course."

In the old days—before Whistler Mountain had a winch cat that could handle The Weasel's impossibly steep slope—that whole section of the course was prepared by hand. Didn't matter how much snow fell the night before, or how much it had rained or thawed or hailed, it was the job of the Weasel crew to make sure that this crucial part of the course was as smooth as a baby's bottom. And the pride that these volunteers took in their job was clearly evident to anyone who took the time to watch them work.

"To stand there, as the racers drop over the lip at 70 mph—and to know that you've had a direct hand in the preparation of the course—it's a feeling that you never get over," says Bob Barnett, the editor of *The Pique*, Whistler's weekly newsmagazine. Barnett worked on his first World Cup downhill at Whistler in 1982. "[The race] didn't even go down The Weasel that year," he says of the only north-side race ever held. "But the camaraderie among the volunteers was so good that I was hooked pretty much right away."

In 1985, in preparation for the Canadian Downhill Championships, Barnett was asked to join a group of elite workers posted to The Weasel.

"It's a unique experience," he explains. "To work for a week solid with a team of like-minded individuals overcoming whatever the weather gods throw at you—rain, snow, slides, whatever—you get pretty close. After all, you're working side by side from six in the morning until six at night."

And these guys were 'core. Most Weasel volunteers would give up just about anything to make sure they could be at Whistler during World Cup week. "We knew our work made a difference to the outcome of the race," adds Barnett. "And that added just enough spice to keep us going when things got rough."

The Weasel Workers' post-downhill party also became something of an event. "We were either celebrating the victors [if all had gone well], or drowning our sorrows [if the race was cancelled]. So no matter what, it was always a big party."

Over time, the image of the Weasel Workers as tough, battle-hardened course warriors came to symbolize the dedication of the vast army of volunteers that was mobilized every time Whistler organized a downhill race. And according to Barnett, that sense of selfless dedication could be traced back to one man.

"Owen Carney has always been a huge inspiration," says Barnett of Whistler's legendary chief-of-course. The father of a former Canadian downhill champion, Carney is the kind of leader who leads by example. "Nobody ever works harder at one of these races than Owen does," adds Barnett.

Today the term Weasel Worker is generally used to describe any volunteer who ends up working on the Dave Murray Downhill course. But the legacy of the name still carries weight among the old-timers.

"You don't know how important these guys are," says Boyd, "until you're flying down The Weasel, hoping and praying that they've done their work properly on the compression below." He laughs. "I always made sure to thank the Weasel Workers properly after every downhill I raced here."

Dave Murray (in red) and early Weasel Workers.

Kye Petersen plays hookie on a
powder day. Whether their names are
Boyd, Janyk or Petersen, Whistler's
young skiers and riders get to practice
their moves on one of the best teaching
grounds in the world.

Determination and discipline.
Britt has never been afraid to set
high standards for herself.

Summer on Blackcomb Glacier is
training ground for some of the
world's best skiers and riders.

I
t's quiet in Whistler Village at this time of the morning. And cool. I quicken my pace a little. My footsteps echo across the empty square. Directly above me, nearly a vertical mile away, rise the glaciated flanks of Blackcomb and Horstman peaks. Already July, yet the big alpine bowls below the summits still seem to be generously endowed with snow. Almost voluptuously so.

By the time I reach the base of Blackcomb's Solar Coaster lift, the sun has begun to pour light over Wedge Mountain to the east. Raucously. Like a giant circus clown with a pailful of colors. Already its warm morning rays hint of more pleasant things to come.

The base area is slowly beginning to fill up. Coaches and technicians, patrollers and lift attendants mill about the loading zone, talking tech talk or big-sport talk. Everyone here seems to know everyone else.

But it's not that surprising. In the summertime, Whistler/Blackcomb serves as a kind of crossroads to the alpine universe—halfpipe stars and new school skiing heroes, Olympic downhill champions and World Cup mogul veterans all pass through here at least once between June and August.

"The glacier is an amazing place for getting the scoop on what's happening in the business," says big-air guru Shane Szocs. "Companies come here to test new products. Athletes come here to develop new moves. This is definitely the place to be in June and July."

The ride up the mountain this morning is magical. Across the valley is Rainbow Mountain, its massive snowfields glistening in the first flood of morning light. To the north is the steep, vertical slice of rock they call Wedge, and beyond that the great massif of Mount Currie, nearly 10,000 feet above sea level.

But as stunning as this is, the view is nothing compared to the wildlife show that is going on below me. I'm not halfway up the Solar Coaster lift when I suddenly spot a big black bear sow on the side of the run with two young cubs in tow. Slowly they move across a patch of clover, grazing contentedly on what passes for bear breakfast around here.

Behind me I hear the excited exclamations of a coaching foursome from Japan. For most Asian visitors to the area, says ski racing coach Keiji Ogawa, a bear sighting is a sign of a successful Canadian holiday. "There is almost a

cult about Canada and bears back in Japan," he says. "The two are inextricably tied." By 9:00 and the first wave of campers, Horstman Glacier is a hive of activity. Courses are set, moguls and jumping ramps are smoothed out and halfpipes are ready for action. Colorful tents advertising everything from ski products to power drinks and energy bars dot the hillside. There is definitely a feeling of festival here.

Like Shane Szocs says, the trends are quick to spot at Whistler in the summer. And the trend today spells snowsports. Bumpers, boardheads, new schoolers and gate bashers all share the area equally—and peacefully. "The scene has really changed in recent years," says veteran camp director, Stephanie Sloan Murray. "It wasn't that long ago that ski camps were a ski-racing thing. Now everyone's doing summer camps."

For a few minutes, I hang at one of the halfpipes watching wild-eyed teens and teen-wannabes throw themselves into the air, each one trying to outdo the one who went before. "You get more from a two-week camp here than you do from a whole season of riding at home," enthuses Long Island rider Tina Maelink during a break in the action. "Great coaching, excellent conditions— and fun riders to train with. It's all there for the taking. You can't help but improve."

Above: **Mogul skiers do their thing.**
Left: **Next year's heroes wait their turn above the halfpipe.**

comes to supporting its own. It's not obvious. And it's not properly celebrated. But it exists nonetheless."

Britt's rise through the national ski racing ranks, if not precociously spectacular, went exactly according to her coaches' plans. "I was never ahead of my age group," she says, "but I was good enough to keep moving forward." There was a group of 12 to 15 very keen, very competitive racers at Whistler in the mid 1990s, she adds. And it created a spirit in the club that was really positive.

"We motivated each other," she explains. "We showed each other how much fun it was to work hard, strive to be the best and then actually achieve those goals."

And always there was Whistler/Blackcomb. Big. And challenging. And brimming with new adventures.

"One of the great things about Whistler," says Britt, "is that the weather here doesn't always cooperate for training. So there are a lot of days when you just go out and freeski. The kids I grew up with here on the racing program—both guys and girls—we're all great freeskiers. They were good racers, for sure. But they were even better skiers. Even today, there's nothing I like better than coming home from racing and hooking up for a few days of *real* skiing with my former teammates."

But while some of her friends slowly drifted out of the racing program, Britt just kept getting stronger. By the time she was 16, Britt was already on the B.C. Team. A year later, she was named to the National Junior Squad. Before she knew it, she was racing World Cup as a full-fledged member of the Canadian Team.

"It goes by so quickly that it's hard to put it all in context sometimes," she admits. "You're focused so much on your own goals that you fail to realize how far you've come." A pause. "But that's a really important part of the mental game. Unless you celebrate the process, you'll never appreciate the product."

It's a philosophy that is constantly tested. Consider her Olympic experience (or nonexperience) in 2002. "To make the Canadian Olympic Team," she explains, "I had to have at least two top-12 finishes in slalom or GS. I already had one from the 2001 season. But I needed another one if I wanted to go to Salt Lake."

As usual for Janyk, everything appeared to be on schedule.

"I was peaking just at the right time," she says. "Although my pre-Christmas races did not go as well as I'd hoped, it really started to come together for me during the January World Cup races."

Twice she finished among the top 15. Twice, the Canadian Olympic Association (COA) refused to bend the rules—even just a little—to let her race at the Games.

"I was so close," she moans. "I could feel myself skiing better and better each race. I knew I could do well at the Olympics. But there was nothing I could do."

What really irks her, she says, is that the COA chose not to exploit Canada's quota fully in the women's slalom and giant slalom event. "They only filled two of the four available spots," she says. "It was devastating for me to see those empty spots and realize that I wouldn't get a chance to compete. I have to admit, it hit me pretty hard."

For some athletes, that defeat could have been the end of the season. Demoralized by the turn of events, many would not have been able to turn their disappointment around and use it to their benefit. But Janyk gritted her teeth and set herself a new goal: "There were a number of Europa Cup events being contested in the Alps while the Olympics were going on. So I decided, 'What the heck. I might as well go back over there and take advantage of the way I'm skiing.' I was still disappointed. But I was pretty determined, too. After all the hard work I'd done, I was not about to let something that was totally out of my control ruin my season."

Indeed. She won the first giant slalom race she entered, finished fifth in the next. And got a couple of strong slalom results in between.

"All the skiers who weren't competing at the Games were there," she says. "The caliber was really high. So it really built up my confidence."

It was also good enough to give her the overall Europa Cup title—not an insignificant achievement given the stature of some of the former winners.

Still, it's not the same as racing in the Olympics. Is she still disappointed she didn't get to compete?

"Next year I want to make some big steps on the World Cup circuit," she says, sidestepping the question. "I've learned so much this year: how to race at this level, how to handle the pressure. In short, how to become better and better as a world-class athlete. And now all I want is the chance to show my stuff."

But what about the 2006 Games in Turin, Italy? Or even the 2010 Olympics at Whistler, if the resort's bid to host the Games goes through? Has she ever thought what that would be like?

She lets the question hang for a moment.

Whistler has always had something of a fixation with the Olympics. Spurned in its bid to become official host in 1968 and disappointed again in 1976, the

Britt gets a congratulatory hug from her coach after kicking butt at the 2002 Canadian Championships. Following in the footsteps of Nancy Greene-Raine, Britt is fast becoming one of Whistler's most visible ambassadors.

competition, it didn't really satisfy local hunger for an Olympic experience. For many, hosting the Games is the only thing that counts. It's the only challenge left.

That's why the 2010 Olympic bid is such a big deal for Whistler. Even though it's no longer part of the official bid title—the International Olympic Committee (IOC) insisted the official bid be named Vancouver 2010, not Vancouver/Whistler 2010—the thought of hosting the world during the quadrennial winter festival still animates the dreams of old-timers and newcomers alike.

"It would be an incredible experience for the community," says Hugh Smythe, onetime president of Whistler/Blackcomb and now president of Intrawest's Resort Operations Group. "To host the world for an event of that size, to live the experience of an Olympic volunteer—I think that could be life-changing for many of us. And it could be the glue that finally binds this town together."

And it's no different for local athletes.

"It's conceivable that I'd still be racing in 2010," says Britt with a faraway look in her eyes. "But I have to admit, I haven't really thought about it much."

It's not that big a stretch, I remind her. After all, she'll only be 29 years old then. And in a sport where the world's best ski racers now extend their careers well into their 30s, that's almost considered the prime of her career.

She smiles again, her dimples betraying her youth again.

"A lot can happen in ski racing in seven years," she says. And then she laughs outright. "A lot can happen in a season. I don't think I could even predict where I'll be in a year, let alone seven. Still, it would be kind of cool to represent your country at the Olympics on your very own home turf."

Her flight is being called. The attendant has already come around once to tell her to get moving. She has to go. We shake hands and I wish her good luck in Europe. "Thank you. I'm looking forward to it myself," she says.

And then she's gone.

community has countered by sending its best and brightest to compete at the Games instead. From Dave Murray to Rob Boyd, Willie Raine to John Smart, Whistler's athletes have always been great ambassadors for the valley. But it's still not the same. Although Ross Rebagliati's snowboarding gold medal in Japan in 1998 showed the world just what Whistlerites could do in

INDEX

PHOTO CREDITS

Cover **Paul Morrison**

Inside Dustjacket **Scott Markewitz**

pp 1 **Scott Markewitz**

pp 2 & 3 **Bruce Rowles**

pp 4 **Greg Griffith**

pp 7 **Gregory Eymundson**

pp 8 & 9 **Damian Cromwell**

pp 10 **Scott Markewitz**

pp 12, (upper left), **Scott Markewitz**

pp 12 & 13 **Blake Jorgensen**

pp 14 **Paul Morrison**

pp 15 **Paul Morrison**

pp 16 **Paul Morrison**

pp 17 **Paul Morrison**

pp 19 **Scott Markewitz**

pp 20 & 21 **Paul Morrison**

pp 22 (upper left) **Whistler Museum Archives**

pp 22 & 23 **Paul Morrison**

pp 24 **Maureen Provencal**

pp 25, 26, 27, 28, 29, 31, 32, 33, **Whistler Museum Archives**

pp 34 **Paul Morrison**

pp 35, 36, 37, 38 **Whistler Museum Archives**

pp 39 **Paul Morrison**

pp 40 & 41 **Maureen Provencal**

pp 42 (upper left) **Wilhelmsen Collection**

pp 42 & 43 **Bryn Hughes**

pp 44 **Wilhelmsen Collection**

pp 45 **Paul Morrison**

pp 46 **Paul Morrison**

pp 47 **Wilhelmsen Collection**

pp 48 **Wilhelmsen Collection**

pp 49 **Paul Morrison**

pp 51 **Whistler Museum Archives**

pp 52 & 53 **Whistler Museum Archives**

pp 54 **Whistler Museum Archives**

pp 55 **Paul Morrison**

pp 56 **Whistler Museum Archives**

pp 57 **Greg Griffith**

pp 58 **Wilhelmsen Collection**

pp 59 **Paul Morrison**

pp 60 & 61 **Bruce Rowles**

pp 62 (upper left) **Fred Lindholm**

pp 62 & 63 **Paul Morrison**

pp 64 **White Museum Achives**

pp 65 **Blake Jorgensen**

pp 66 **Eric Berger**

pp 67 **Ski Magazine Archives**

pp 69 **Scott Markewitz**

pp 70 & 71 **Paul Morrison**

pp 72 **Blake Jorgensen**

pp 73 **Paul Morrison**

pp 74 **Maureen Provencal**

pp 75 **Ski Magazine Archives**

pp 76 **Courtesy of Trudy Alder**

pp 77 **Greg Griffith**

pp 78 & 79 **Paul Morrison**

pp 80 (upper left) **Paul Morrison**

pp 80 & 81 **Paul Morrison**

pp 82 **Collection of Hugh Smythe**

pp 83 **Whistler Museum Archives**

pp 84 **Greg Griffith**

pp 85 **Paul Morrison**

pp 87 **Whistler Blackcomb Collection**

pp 88 **Collection of Hugh Smythe**

pp 89 **Collection of Hugh Smythe**

pp 90 & 91 **Paul Morrison**

pp 92 **Bruce Rowles**

pp 93 **Chris Speedie**

pp 94 **David Perry**

pp 95 **Jeremy Hanrahan**

pp 96 **Paul Morrison**

pp 98 & 99 **Eric Berger**

pp 100 (upper left) **Paul Morrison**

pp 100 & 101 **Greg Griffith**

pp 102 **Paul Ryan**

pp 103 (left) **Whistler Mountain Archives**

pp 103 (right) **Ski Magazine Archives**

pp 104 **Ski Magazine Archives**

pp 105 **Al Safrata**

pp 107 **Ski Magazine Archives**

pp 108, 109 **Al Raine Collection**

pp 110 **Whistler Blackcomb Collection**

pp 111 **Ski Magazine Archives**

pp 112 **Greg Griffith**

pp 114 **Greg Griffith**

pp 115 **Paul Morrison**

pp 116 & 117 **Toshi Kawano**

pp 118 **Paul Morrison**

pp 119 **Paul Morrison**

pp 120 & 121 **Paul Morrison**

pp 122 (upper left) **David Dolsen**

pp 122 & 123 **Paul Morrison**

pp 124 **Vincent Massey Collection**

pp 125 **Paul Morrison**

pp 126 **Vincent Massey Collection**

pp 128 & 129 **Paul Morrison**

pp 130 **Blake Jorgensen**

pp 131 **Paul Morrison**

pp 133 **Vincent Massey Collection**

pp 134 **Jonathan Selkowitz**

pp 135 **Bruce Rowles**

pp 136 **Vincent Massey Collection**

pp 137 **Paul Morrison**

pp 138 & 139 **Eric Berger**

pp 140 (upper left) **Blake Jorgensen**

pp 140 & 141 **Paul Morrison**

pp 142 **Damian Cromwell**

pp 143 **Cathy Jewett Collection**

pp 144 **Scott Markewitz**

pp 145 (top) **Scott Markewitz,** (bottom) **Paul Morrison**

pp 146 **Paul Morrison**

pp 147 **Cathy Jewett Collection**

pp 149 **Gail Morrison Collection**

pp 150 **Cathy Jewett Collection**

pp 151 **Paul Morrison**

pp 152 & 153 **Maureen Provencal**

pp 154 **Scott Markewitz**

pp 155 **Greg Griffith**

pp 156 **Gail Morrison Collection**

pp 157 **Doug Stern**

pp 158 & 159 **Greg Griffith**

pp 160 (upper left) **Paul Morrison**

pp 160 & 161 **Murray Coates**

pp 162 (right) **Boyd Family Collection**

pp 162 (left) **Don Weixl**

pp 163 **Paul Morrison**

pp 164 & 165 **Paul Morrison**

pp 166 **Paul Morrison**

pp 167 **Boyd Family Collection**

pp 168 **Paul Morrison**

pp 169 **Paul Morrison**

pp 170 **Maureen Provencal**

pp 171 **Paul Morrison**

pp 173 **Boyd Family Collection**

pp 174 **Whistler Museum Archives**

pp 175 **Bryn Hughes**

pp 176 **Joyce Alvavez**

pp 177 **Toshi Kawano**

pp 178 & 179 **Paul Decarie**

pp 180 (upper left) **Eric Berger**

pp 180 & 181 **Blake Jorgensen**

pp 182, 183 **Eric Berger**

pp 185 **Eric Berger**

pp 186 **Blake Jorgensen**

pp 187 **Eric Berger**

pp 188 & 189 **Jia Condon**

pp 190 **Bruce Rowles**

pp 191 **?????**

pp 192 **Bruce Rowles**

pp 193 (top) **Paul Morrison**

pp 193 (bottom) **Jonathan Selkowitz**

pp 194 **Ace MacKay-Smith**

pp 195 **Bruce Rowles**

pp 196 **Blake Jorgensen**

pp 197 **Bruce Rowles**

pp 198 **Paul Morrison**

pp 199 **Blake Jorgensen**

pp 200 & 201 **Greg Eymundson**

pp 202 (upper left) **Courtesy of Andree Janyk**

pp 202 & 203 **Greg Griffith**

pp 204 **Malcolm Carmichael**

pp 205 **Courtesy of Andree Janyk**

pp 206 **Scott Markewitz**

pp 207 (both) **Bonny Makarewicz**

pp 208 **Bonny Makarewicz**

pp 210 **Courtesy of Andree Janyk**

pp 211 **Toshi Kawano**

pp 212 **Owen Carney Collection**

pp 213 **Bruce Rowles**

pp 214 & 215 **Bonny Makarewicz**

pp 216 **Bruce Rowles**

pp 217 (both) **Bruce Rowles**

pp 219 **Malcolm Carmichael**

pp 220 & 221 **Craig Mutch**

pp 226 & 227 **Paul Morrison**

Back Cover (top) **Maureen Provencal**

Back Cover (bottom) **Greg Griffith**